BUILDING LAW REPORTS

EDITOR IN CHIEF

Humphrey LLoyd, QC, MA, LLB (Dub)
Barrister; Recorder of the Crown Court

EDITORS

Nicholas Baatz, MA, BCL (Oxon)
Barrister

David Streatfeild-James, BA (Oxon)
Barrister

VOLUME
54

LONGMAN

Longman Group UK Limited,
Longman House, Burnt Mill, Harlow, Essex CM20 2JE, England
and Associated Companies throughout the World.

First published 1991

ISSN 0141-5875

ISBN 0 582 08132 7

Printed and bound in Great Britain
by Bath Press, Bath

Contents

Introduction

Computer Systems and Engineering Plc v *John Lelliott (Ilford) Ltd* (at page 1) is a decision of the Court of Appeal on the meaning of the word "flood" in the list of risks set out in Clause 22 of the 1980 JCT Form of Building Contract. The flood had arisen as a result of the discharge of the fire protection system which had been caused by negligence on the part of a sub-contractor. The Court of Appeal held that neither "flood" nor "bursting of pipes" covered the circumstances of the case so that the employer was not liable for the risk.

The next case is a decision of the British Columbia Court of Appeal: *Edgeworth Construction Ltd* v *N D Lea & Associates Limited* (at page 11). That Court held that consulting engineers were not liable to contractors for losses allegedly incurred as a result of the performance of work in accordance with a design prepared by the engineers since the engineers owed no duty of care as they had only prepared the design for the Highways Ministry who had taken it over. The engineers were not thereafter responsible for the use made of the design. The Court also considered and followed, although for reasons which were not completely clear, the difficult case of *Pacific Associates Inc* v *Baxter* [1990] QB 993; 44 BLR 3.

Badgerhill Properties Ltd v *Cottrell* (at page 23) is included, notwithstanding its rather special facts, as it illustrates a common-sense approach to the resolution of technical problems in the formation of contracts: the plaintiffs had misdescribed themselves in their transaction with the defendant and as a result of being in financial difficulties the defendant alleged that she was liable only to the director or agent who had made the contracts with her. The Court of Appeal held that the contracts had been made with the company for reasons which appear from the judgment.

Two cases follow on exercise of the Court's power to remit awards to arbitrators where there has been error in the proceedings. *Blexen Ltd* v *G. Percy Trentham* (at page 37) was concerned with a decision by an arbitrator on costs. The Court held that it had no jurisdiction to remit. As the award was a reasoned one, it was capable only of challenge only under Section 1(3) of the Arbitration Act 1979. In *King* v *Thomas McKenna Ltd* (at page 48) an award on costs was however remitted to the arbitrator for reconsideration as it had been made without knowledge that a sealed offer had been made so that the case had not been properly adjudicated.

Du Bosky & Partners v *Shearwater Property Holdings plc* (at page 71) the Court rejected an argument on behalf of the plaintiffs that under a contractual provision for termination they were entitled to recover more than the amounts then accrued to be due on the basis that the agreement apparently failed to provide for the plaintiffs' fees in the event of the termination and before full entitlement had been earned.

Finally, in *Watts* v *Morrow* (at page 86) the Court of Appeal declined to depart from its long-standing decision in *Phillips* v *Ward* [1956] 1 WLR 571; 4 BLR 142 and dismissed an appeal on a decision of His Honour Judge Bowsher in which he had held that a plaintiff might recover the cost of putting the house right rather than the loss of value occasioned by negligence in a pre-purchase survey. The effect of this decision is also to over-rule the same Judge's decision in *Syrett* v *Carr and Neave* (included in this volume for convenience at page 121, as a Note. The Court of Appeal also gave valuable guidance as to the assessment of damages for loss and inconvenience confining them to those instances where there had also been physical discomfort or inconvenience and not merely mental distress.

1 Atkin Building HJLL
Gray's Inn NB
London WC1R 5BQ DS-J

COMPUTER & SYSTEMS ENGINEERING plc v JOHN LELLIOTT (ILFORD) Ltd and Another

5 December 1990 *Court of Appeal*

Purchas, Taylor and Beldam LJJ

Contract – JCT Private edition, 1980, Clause 22 – "Storm, tempest, flood" – Whether water discharged from sprinkler system was "flood"

On 16 September 1983 the first defendant ("Lelliott") was employed by the plaintiff ("Case") under JCT 1980 contract conditions for work to the ground and first floors of Case's premises at Caxton Way, Watford. Part of the work involved the installation of steel purlins to support a new false ceiling and services. Lelliott subcontracted this work to the second defendant ("Stoddart"). The terms of the subcontract were materially identical to the contract between Lelliott and Case.

On 11 December 1983, one of Stoddart's employees let slip a purlin which fell and sheared off part of the existing fire protection system. In consequence 1,600 gallons of water were discharged, damaging Case's property.

On 10 July 1986 Case started proceedings against Lelliott and Stoddart, and subsequently Lelliott served a contribution notice on Stoddart claiming to be entitled to an indemnity in the event that Lelliott was held liable to Case. Lelliott (and Stoddart) argued that the damage was caused by a peril which, by virtue of Clause 22 of the JCT conditions (set out in full at pages 5-7 below) was at Case's sole risk. It was accepted that Stoddart's liability to Lelliott was contingent upon this issue, and that if Lelliott were liable to Case, Stoddart would be liable to indemnify Lelliott. The judge held that the damage was within the words of Clause 22, and was not caused by a risk which Case had accepted. Accordingly, he gave judgment for Case in the action, and for Lelliott in the contribution proceedings. Stoddart appealed.

***HELD**, dismissing the appeal,*

(1) On their proper construction, Clauses 20.2 and 22 of the contract did not limit the risks assumed by an employer under the JCT 1980 contract to loss or damage not caused by the fault of the contractor or subcontractor.

Scottish Special Housing Association v *Wimpey Construction UK Ltd.* [1986] 1 WLR 895; 34 BLR 1 *applied*

(2) The word "flood" in Clause 22 of the contract did not cover the discharge of the sprinkler system.

Per Beldam LJ:

> "In the context of this contract, "flood", in my view, imports the invasion of the property, which is at the employer's risk, by a large volume of water caused by a rapid accumulation or sudden release of water from an external source, usually but not necessarily confined to the result of a natural phenomenon such as a storm, tempest or downpour."

(3) The words "bursting of pipes" in Clause 22 of the contract did not cover the breaking of pipes in the circumstances of this case.

Per Beldam LJ:

> "... I have no doubt that in this context the bursting of tanks, apparatus or pipes is confined to the rupture of tanks, apparatus or pipe from within, typically caused by the exertion of forces, such as expansion or pressure within the pipe itself ..."

S Jones appeared for Stoddart, instructed by Lawrence Walsh
John Slater QC and S F Coles appeared for Case, instructed by Jarvis and Bannister

Commentary

As noted in the commentary to *Scottish Special Housing Association* v *Wimpey Construction Ltd* (1985) 34 BLR1, a contractual provision which relieves a contractor or subcontractor from the consequences of his own negligence may not be particularly attractive for employers and their insurers. Equally, while (of course) it is a matter for the parties (and their insurers) to stipulate where the risk of negligence is to lie, the courts are unlikely to be sympathetic to attempts to extend the ambit of provisions such as Clause 22: a provision which stipulates that a party is not liable for the consequences of its negligence, ought, as a matter of principle, to be construed narrowly.

The decision of the Court of Appeal in this case illustrates this point as well as providing a useful general analysis of the Clause 22 perils. A discharge of a fire sprinkler system of the size in this case — 1,600 gallons of water — might in a loose sense be regarded as a flood, but not surprisingly Beldam LJ was not attracted to this construction. A "flood" in the context of Clause 22 was in his opinion quite clearly an external — and probably naturally occurring — event.

As Beldam LJ pointed out although the question in the case was one of construction and not causation, had the purlin fallen through the floor and damaged valuable computer equipment the subcontractor would clearly have been liable and the additional factor of the sprinkler system ought not to have affected that position.

COMPUTER & SYSTEMS ENGINEERING plc v JOHN LELLIOTT (ILFORD) Ltd and Another

5 December 1990 *Court of Appeal*

Purchas, Taylor and Beldam LJJ

PURCHAS LJ: I will invite Beldam LJ to deliver the first judgment.

BELDAM LJ: The second defendants, E W G Stoddart Ltd, appeal to this court from the judgment of His Honour Judge Iain Black (sitting as an additional judge of the High Court) given on 12 May 1989 in favour of the plaintiffs against the first defendants, in the sum of £269,000 with costs, to be taxed if not agreed and judgment for the first defendants against the second defendants on a contribution notice for a full indemnity.

The plaintiffs, usually known by the abbreviated name of Case plc, were the owners and occupiers of the first and ground floor of premises at Caxton Way, Watford, Hertfordshire. In this judgment I shall refer to them as the "employers", for so they were described in a contract dated 16 September 1983, by which they engaged the first defendants, John Lelliott (Ilford) Ltd (referred to as the "contractor"), for the purpose of making alterations to and fitting out works on the first and ground floor of their premises at Caxton Way and erecting a service building there.

The contractors agreed to carry out and complete works in accordance with the drawings and specifications referred to for the sum of £586,450. The contract was in the Standard Form of Building Contract, 1980 edition, of the Joint Contracts Tribunal, Private Edition, Without Quantities.

Part of the works which the contractor had undertaken required the installation of approximately one hundred and forty steel purlins in the existing building to support new services and a false ceiling. The purlins were twenty feet in length and weighed over twenty-one kilograms and had to be placed under the gable floor of the existing building, but above the sprinkler system installed there.

The contractors sub-contracted the work of installing the purlins to the second defendants, the appellants (E W G Stoddart Limited), who were steel erectors. They agreed to carry out the work of erecting the purlins under a standard form of sub-contract, dated 27 October 1983, for the sum of £4,472, less discount. The conditions of the sub-contract mirrored those in the main contract.

Shortly after midday on 11 December 1983, whilst he was engaged in the work of erecting the purlins, Mr Chase, an employee of the sub-contractors, was trying to position one of the purlins when it slipped from its support at one end and fell to the ground. Unfortunately, as it fell, it sheared through and broke off a pipe which was part of the existing installation of the fire protection sprinkler system. The system discharged and water was sprayed from the broken end of the pipe. It eventually seeped through the floor and on to the employer's property stored on the ground floor, causing damage amounting in all to £164,000.

The judge found that until the system was turned off by a representative of the manufacturer of the sprinkler system, who was providentially at hand, about 600 to 800 gallons of water escaped. Thereafter a further quantity flowed out until the system was empty. In total the judge found that about 1,600 gallons had been discharged from the system.

On 10 July 1986 the employers issued the writ in this action claiming that sum and interest from the contractor and sub-contractor. At the trial the sub-contractor contended that it was not to blame and that the employer had caused or contributed to the loss that was suffered by his own fault. The judge, however, rejected those contentions and found, as on the evidence appears inevitable, that the loss was entirely caused by the fault of the sub-contractor.

The contractors by their defence contended that even if the damage suffered by the employers was due to fault on the part of the sub-contractor, for which they were responsible, nevertheless the loss or damage which the employer had suffered arose from a peril which, by the terms of the contract, was at the sole risk of the employer himself. In view of the coincidence of the terms of the contract and the sub-contract it is accepted by the parties that if the employer's loss arose from a peril for which they had accepted the sole risk they cannot recover against the sub-contractors. Accordingly, in this appeal, the sub-contractors have relied upon and argued the case raised in the contractor's defence.

The clause in the contract relied upon by the contractor is clause 22C 1.1. It reads:

> "The existing structures together with the contents thereof owned by him or for which he is responsible and the Works and all unfixed

materials and goods, delivered to placed on or adjacent to the Works and intended for incorporation therein (but excluding temporary buildings, plant, tools and equipment owned or hired by the Contractor or any sub-contractor) shall be at the sole risk of the Employer as regards loss or damage by the Clause 22 Perils and the Employer shall maintain adequate insurance against loss or damage by the Clause 22 Perils."

The clause 22 perils are defined in clause 1.3 of the contract as:

"... fire, lightning, explosion, storm, tempest, flood, bursting or overflowing of water tanks, apparatus or pipes, earthquake, aircraft and other aerial devices or articles dropped therefrom, riot and civil commotion, (excluding any loss or damage caused by ironising radiations ... etc."

It was contended by the contractor that damage to the employer's property was caused, either by flood or by bursting of apparatus or pipes, and that consequently, notwithstanding that the damage was also caused by the negligence of the sub-contractor, that property was at the risk of the employer from those perils during the period of the contract.

The judge held that on the true construction of the contract the event for which the sub-contractor was responsible was not a clause 22 peril and consequently gave judgment for the employer against the contractor and sub-contractor. The sub-contractor now appeals, contending that the judge wrongly construed the provisions of the contract and that on the true construction of the clause 22 perils, the damage suffered by the employer was at his sole risk. The issue, therefore, is whether the event which occurred at the employer's premises on 13 December 1983, causing their property to be damaged by water, amounted to a flood or bursting of apparatus or pipes within the ambit of the risks accepted by the employers as theirs.

Before the learned judge and before us both the sub-contractor and the employer relied upon cases in which the courts have construed the word "flood" and the sub-contractor relied on a decision on the meaning of the clause in the contract in an earlier edition of a JCT contract for local authorities. The assistance to be gained from such cases has to be tempered by the cautionary advice of Lord Atkin *In re Calf and the Sun Insurance Company* [1920] 2 KB 366 at page 382, in which he says:

"It was a pure question of construction, and on a question of construction I protest against one case being treated as an authority in another unless the language and the circumstances are substantially identical."

In his able argument for the sub-contractors, Mr Jones has pointed to two respects in which the judge in construing the clause 22 perils fell into error by relying on immaterial matters. The first was in basing his conclusion that the employers' damage was not caused by flood because the ordinary Englishman would have said that it was caused by the dropping of the purlin on the pipe. I agree with Mr Jones that even if this would have been the reaction of the ordinary person to the events in question, it did not determine the meaning of the word "flood" in this clause of the contract; the judge still had to consider whether the consequent escape of water was within the proper meaning to be given to "flood".

Secondly, in arriving at his conclusion the judge said that no court should be astute to construe the clause 22 perils in a way which had the effect of absolving a wholly and solely guilty tortfeasor from the consequences of his wrong, but that was the purpose of the exception to the indemnity otherwise given under clause 20 by the contractor, for the consequences of his fault or the fault of those for whom he was answerable and was the reason why the employer under the contract accepted as his the risk of damage to his property by those perils.

The judge, having based his conclusion wrongly, as I think, on those considerations, it is now necessary to consider whether, properly construed, the clause 22 perils included the risk of the event which led to the employer's loss or damage.

The clauses in the contract have to be construed against the background of an agreement for the carrying out of work by the contractor on premises of the employer in which the parties to the contract had in clauses 20, 21 and 22C 1.1, sought to divide between them responsibility for accidents and damage occurring during the carrying out of the contract and had made provision for insurance against the risk of injury and damage being caused whilst the works were in progress. Thus in clause 20, entitled "Injury to persons and property and Employers' indemnity", the contractors are made liable for and undertake to indemnify the employer against any liability, claim or proceedings in respect of personal injury to or death of anyone arising out of the execution of the works, unless due to the act of the employer or someone for whom he is responsible.

By clause 20.2 it is provided:

> "Except for such loss or damage as is at the sole risk of the Employer under clause ... 22C ... the Contractor shall be liable for, and shall indemnify the Employer against, any ... loss ... or damage whatsoever to any property real or personal in so far as such injury or damage arises out of or in the course of or by reason of the carrying out of the Works, and provided ... that the same is due to any negligence ... of the Contractor, ... or any sub-contractor."

Clause 21 required the contractor to maintain the necessary insurances to cover his liability or the sub-contractor's liability in respect of damage to property etc. The loss or damage excepted from the contractor's indemnity is that declared by clause 22 to be at the sole risk of the employer. Clause 22C 1.1 requires the employer to maintain adequate insurance against loss or damage by those perils. The words, "storm, tempest and flood", are standard perils frequently found appearing together in policies of insurance against damage to property. They have from time to time been interpreted by the court and it is consistent with Lord Atkin's advice to consider the construction which has been placed on the words in that context. Equally, it seems to me, that where the wording of an earlier edition of a similar standard form of building contract has been considered by a court and where it contained provisions identical to those of the instant case, it is not only permissible, it is essential in the cause of consistency to consider the construction put upon the clause in that case.

In *Scottish Special Housing Association* v *Wimpey Construction UK Ltd* [1986] 1 WLR 995; 34 BLR 1 the conditions of the JCT standard form of local authority building contract, 1963 edition, as revised in 1977, were construed by the House of Lords. Clause 18.2 of those conditions contained the same exception as that contained in clause 20(2) of this contract and in clause 20C provided for the existing structures and contents to be at the sole risk of the employer as regards loss or damage by fire, lightning, explosion, storm, tempest, flood, bursting or overflowing of water tanks, apparatus or pipes, earthquake, aircraft and other aerial devices or articles dropped therefrom.

The loss in that case arose from a fire caused by the contractor's negligence. The employer had argued that the exception in clause 18.2 of the conditions only applied to loss or damage and the perils referred to which were not caused by the negligence of the contractor or sub-contractor.

Lord Keith, in a judgment with which all their Lordships concurred, pointed out that in the case of fire, the peril in question in that case, no differentiation was made between fire due to the negligence of the contractor and fire due to other causes. He continued:

> "The remainder of the catalogue of perils includes some which could not possibly be caused by the negligence of the contractor, such as storm, tempest and earthquake, but others which might be, such as explosion, flood and the bursting or overflowing of water pipes. There is imposed upon the employer an obligation to ensure against loss or damage by all these perils, in quite general terms. I have found it impossible to resist the conclusion that is is intended that the

> employer shall bear the whole risk of damage by fire, including fire caused by the negligence of the contractor or that of sub-contractors. The exception introduced by the opening words of clause 18(2) must have the effect that certain damage caused by the negligence of the contractor or sub-contractors, for which in the absence of these words the contractor would be liable, is not to result in liability on his part. The nature of such damage is to be found in clause 20[C], which refers in general terms to damage by fire to the existing structures. No sensible content can be found for the words of exception in clause 18(2) if they are not read as referring to damage of the nature described in clause 20(C)."

I would therefore reject the construction of clauses 22 and 20(2) in the present contract which confined the exception for loss or damage at the sole risk of the employer, to "loss or damage caused by the perils referred to which was not caused by the fault of the contractor or sub-contractor". Such a construction would be inconsistent with the exception from the indemnity for loss or damage caused by negligence, omission or default of the contractor.

The question, whether the loss or damage to his property sustained by the employer arose from one of the excepted perils, still remains to be considered. In this context the words, "storm, tempest or flood", appearing in a policy of insurance were construed by this court in *Young* v *Sun Alliance and London Insurance Ltd* [1976] 3 All ER 561. The court there held that the juxtaposition of the three words, "storm, tempest or flood", was significant and that even though in colloquial parlance "flooding" or "flooded" might be used to describe any substantial ingress of water into a building, in this context "flood" refers to an inundation emanating from a natural phenomenon and which has some element of violence, suddenness or largeness about it.

In the present case the words "storm, tempest and flood", are followed by "bursting or overflowing of water tanks, apparatus or pipes". This express reference to risks associated with and emanating from an installation used for the collection, storage and distribution of water, generally located in premises, reinforces the restrictive meaning to be given to the word "flood", for if inundation from any source or cause was encompassed by the word "flood", no content would remain for the words which follow. As Lord Keith remarked, there have been many cases in which flooding of premises and damage originating from a natural downpour have been contributed to by a blockage of drains, downpipes or culverts due to fault on the part of the contractor. Moreover in my view since the risks associated with water tanks, apparatus or pipes are expressly confined to bursting or overflowing, any flooding of the premises from water eminating from such an installation was intended to be confined to an occurrence of that nature.

In the context of this contract "flood", in my view, imports the invasion of the property, which is at the employer's risk, by a large volume of water caused by a rapid accumulation or sudden release of water from an external source, usually but not necessarily confined to the result of a natural phenomenon such as a storm, tempest or downpour. I conclude that the event caused by Mr Chase was not a flood because neither in extent or origin was it within that meaning.

It has been argued that the consequences of the sub-contractor's actions in this case amounted to the bursting of pipes or apparatus. Mr Jones has argued that "bursting of pipes" should be given a wide rather than a narrow meaning and he has criticised the judge for adopting the submission of the employers that the word in the context was used intransitively. As he says, it is possible for a person to burst a pipe or, for example, a balloon by puncturing it from the outside and if the contents are under pressure such an event might properly be described as "a burst". However that may be, I have no doubt that in this context the bursting of tanks, apparatus or pipes is confined to the rupture of tank, apparatus or pipe from within typically caused by the exertion of forces, such as expansion or pressure within the vessel or pipe itself and I would reject the meaning of "bursting of pipes" so expanded as to cover the event caused by the negligence of Mr Chase in this case.

I am reinforced in my view of the construction of clause 22 perils by the fact that clause 22.1[C] required insurance against the risk of damage to property caused by those perils and that if a policy was obtained by the employer which used these words to define the risks insured against they would be accorded that meaning. The parties clearly must be taken to have intended that the employer would effect the policy against the risks described and a different construction could not rationally be given to the word "flood" in the contract from that which it bore in the policy.

In my judgment the peril of the breaking or shearing off of the sprinkler pipe by dropping a heavy purlin upon it was not one which under the terms of this contract was at the sole risk of the employer and the contractor was liable to indemnify the employer against the damage caused. I would dismiss the appeal.

TAYLOR LJ: I agree.

PURCHAS LJ: I also agree that this appeal fails for the reasons given by Beldam LJ.

EDGEWORTH CONSTRUCTION Ltd v N D LEA & ASSOCIATES Ltd EDGEWORTH CONSTRUCTION Ltd v WALJI and Others

18 February 1991 *British Columbia Court of Appeal*

Lambert, MacDonald and Hollinrake JJA

Negligence – Mis-statements – Whether engineers liable to contractors for errors in tender documents.

In October 1977 the defendant engineers who were consulting engineers or engineers employed by them were engaged by the British Columbia Ministry of Highways to design a road. They prepared specifications and drawings and submitted them to the Ministry which incorporated them in tender documents. The plaintiff contractors tendered for and were in November 1979 awarded a contract to build 6.8 km of the road for C$6,985,245.

The defendants were not named as the engineer in the contract and had no control over the use made by the Ministry of the documents containing their design.

In the event the plaintiffs were paid C$19,444,250 under the contract and claimed a further C$21,694,211. In November 1986 the plaintiffs commenced proceedings (to which all the defendants became parties in two actions) by which the plaintiffs alleged that the design had been negligently prepared and that the defendants were liable for negligent mis-statements arising out of the preparation of the tender drawings, plans and specifications which had led to the plaintiffs incurring substantial additional expenditure.

The defendants applied for summary judgment on the basis that they owed no duty of care to the plaintiffs, for which purpose all the allegations of fact pleaded in the statement of claim were assumed to be true. Meredith J granted the defendants' application and dismissed the actions ((1989) 37 CLR 152; [1990] BCWLD 214). The plaintiffs appealed.

***HELD**, dismissing the appeal:*

(1) A claim for negligent mis-statement depends on the existence of a duty of care, and such a duty arises from foreseeability, reliance and proximity. There must be foreseeability of economic loss being caused to someone in a specific class which is put at risk by the carelessness in question. Reliance must be justifiable and reasonable and must be foreseeable by the person whose careless misrepresentation creates the risk. Proximity means more than physical connection. It encompasses all the circumstances that cause one person to depend on another and in such a way as to cause that other to bear responsibility for carelessly-created risks.

(2) When the Ministry of Highways incorporated the defendants' design, plans and specification in the tender documents, they became representations of the Ministry to prospective bidders. They ceased to be representations of the defendants, at least as regards proximity for the purposes of a duty of care with respect to economic loss. The whole question of flaws in the design, plans and specifications was an appropriate matter for the contract between the plaintiffs and the Ministry. The defendants had no direct relationship with the plaintiffs and no opportunity to define what risks it was prepared to assume. The defendants had no control over the contents of the contract between the Ministry and the plaintiffs and, in all the circumstances, the necessary relationship of proximity essential to the plaintiffs' claim was absent.

Caparo Industries plc v *Dickman* [1990] 2 WLR 358 *followed; Pacific Associates Inc* v *Baxter* [1990] QB 993; (1988) 44 BLR 33 *followed*

J P Taylor QC and J R Lysyk appeared for the plaintiffs
N H Smith and J Hand appeared for the defendants

Commentary
This decision is a useful one and will provide the basis of much discussion. At one level it illustrates that at least one Commonwealth appellate court prefers to follow the most recent decision of the House of Lords in *Murphy* v *Brentwood District Council* [1990] 1 AC 398 and, thereby, the view of Brennan J in *Sutherland Shire Council* v *Heyman* (1985) 60 ALR 1 at pages 43-44 as adopted by the House of Lords in *Caparo Industries* v *Dickman* [1990] 2 WLR 358. It therefore leaves the New Zealand Courts even more exposed: see *Mount Albert Borough* v *Johnson* [1979] 2 NZLR 234.

On another level it indicates the likely attitude of the courts not only in Canada but also in other countries outside England to the question left unresolved by *Pacific Associates Inc* v *Baxter* (1988) 40 BLR 33.

As Lambert JA mentioned in his judgment, there has been a long line of cases in Canada in which it has been held that an engineer may be liable in law if the tender documents were negligently prepared. Such liability arose on the basis of what was thought to be the effect in *Hedley Byrne* v *Heller & Partners Ltd* [1964] AC 465. Thus, for example, in *Walter Cabot Construction Ltd* v *R* (1974) 44 DLR (3d) 82 it was held that the engineers were under a duty of care to tenderers since they must have known the tenderers would rely upon the tender documents, particularly where the contracts did not require the contractor to satisfy itself about sub-surface conditions. That approach was followed by R E Holland J in *Brown & Huston Ltd* v *York* (1983) 5 CLR 240 — a decision of the Ontario Supreme Court (High Court of Justice). He there found, amongst other things, that a contractor had relied on the tender documents in preparing its tender on the basis that there was no problem in dealing with groundwater when tendering for the construction of an underground pumping station for the City of York. The judge said: "I have come to the conclusion that there was reasonable reliance on the lack of information concerning a water condition so as to bring the case within the principles enunciated in *Hedley Byrne* v *Heller & Partners* ...". A similar opinion was adopted by Henry J in *Cardinal Construction Ltd* v *Brockville* (1984) 4 CLR 149 (also in the Ontario High Court) — see pages 192-195. In another province (Alberta) an architect was held liable to a contractor for wrong levels: *Joslyn* v *Olsen Contractors* (1976) 1 Abta (2nd) 174. Mr I N Duncan Wallace QC thought this correct in principle as a *Hedley Byrne* negligent misrepresentation (see 21 BLR 5).

In *Auto Concrete Kerb Ltd* v *South Nation River Conservation Authority* (1988) 30 CLR 245, Yates J (also in the Ontario High Court) held the defendant engineers liable on the same basis to a contractor. This is a case of some interest: the plaintiffs had tendered to control and regulate flooding on the South Nation river. The material from the river was to be removed by a suction dredging method to which the defendant employer later raised objection. The plaintiffs were allowed by the engineers to continue the work only if a different method of dredging was used as a result of which the plaintiffs commenced actions against both the employer and the engineer. Yates J held that suction dredging was an acceptable method of excavation and would have been within the contemplation of a competent engineer in the preparation of tender documents for the project; that the tender documents for the project were improperly prepared "in that they contained no restrictions or reservations with regard to the method of excavation" and therefore the engineers were negligent in that regard. He also held that the engineers knew or ought to have known that the contractors would rely upon the information supplied in the invitation to tender and a failure to include all relevant information constituted a negligent misrepresentation.

However, Lambert JA in the British Columbia Court of Appeal dismissed these decisions on the basis that in *Brown & Huston* and in *Auto Concrete Kerb Ltd* "the question of the liability of the engineer as an independent liability does not bear the hallmarks of having been thoroughly argued". He also thought that "a good deal has happened in this area of law since *Cardinal Construction Ltd* v *Brockville*". He went on to say that one of the most important things that has happened was the decision in *Pacific Associates Inc* v *Baxter*.

Yet, as was pointed out in the Commentary to *Pacific Associates Inc* v *Baxter* (see 46 BLR pages 36-37) it is not easy to discern the principle for which that case might be authority since each member of the English Court of Appeal decided the appeal on slightly different grounds — disregarding the special clause 86 by which the engineer was declared not to be "personally liable for the acts or obligations under the contract . . ."

More relevant, in our view, are the reasons given by Lambert JA for denying a duty of care in the circumstances in which Edgeworth Construction had tendered, namely that any representations that were made were not made by the engineer but by the engineer's employer, the Ministry, and the fact that Edgeworth had the opportunity (perhaps a notional one) to redistribute the risks inherent in tendering for a project for which the design might contain flaws. On the other hand the designing engineers (who were not the engineer under the contract) "had no opportunity to define with Edgeworth Construction the risks that it was prepared to assume, if any, and the risks it was not prepared to assume, in relation to Edgeworth" (see page 21).

This therefore leaves open the questions: first, of the liability of an engineer to a contractor where such factors are not present (eg when the engineer has control over the tender documents and where the contractor had no option but to tender on the basis sought) and, second, where an engineer has had specific communications with the contractor prior to tendering when a true *Hedley Byrne* relationship might arise. Thus there may be circumstances in which an engineer will be held to have assumed, voluntarily or otherwise, responsibility to a contractor when tendering. It will be recalled that in *Dillingham Construction* v *Downs* [1972] 2 NSWLR 49; 13 BLR 97 the contractor's claim failed because (amongst other reasons) the contractor was held by the contract to have assumed responsibility (and not the engineer).

Even though Lambert JA referred to several precedents (see page 20) he did not refer to *Vermont Construction* v *Beatson* (1976) 67 DLR (3rd) 95 in which the Supreme Court of Canada had held an architect not liable in law to a contractor for losses due to an inaccurate drawing. Meredith J in the court below had, however, done so and relied on it in his judgment (see 37 CLR 163), drawing attention to the fact that the contract exonerated the owner for delay. He quoted part of the judgment of Pidgeon J in which he had said that the contractor's remedy against the architect was limited and that by the contract it had been agreed that it would have no claim against the owner: "How then could it be able to make a claim against the architect?" Perhaps Lambert JA thought that *Vermont Construction* was insufficiently clear to follow.

EDGEWORTH CONSTRUCTION Ltd v N D LEA & ASSOCIATES Ltd
EDGEWORTH CONSTRUCTION Ltd v WALJI and Others

18 February 1991 *British Columbia Court of Appeal*

Lambert, Macdonald and Hollinrake JJA

LAMBERT JA delivered the judgment of the court: The question in this appeal [from 37 CLR 152, [1990] BCWLD 214] is whether an engineering firm, engaged by the Crown to do the design work for a highway construction project, including the preparation of plans and specifications to be incorporated in the tender documents and contract documents, owes a duty of care to the contractor who is ultimately awarded the construction contract, in relation to the risk of economic loss caused by alleged careless inaccuracies in the design and in the plans and specifications.

In October 1977 the Ministry of Highways, by letter, "assigned" the design project for 19.4 km of highway relocation near the Revelstoke dam site to N D Lea & Associates ("N D Lea"), described as "the consultant". Among the tasks to be undertaken by the consultant were these:

> The Consultant will:
>
> 2. Prepare detail construction plans, profiles, cross-section, mass diagrams, and supplementary drawings including working drawings as necessary, with complete detail and geometry as required to lay out and construct the roadway facility, including intersections, surfacing, base and sub-base, sub-grade, drainage courses and structures, stripping, seeding and other right of way treatment, fencing, and including borrow areas, disposal areas, surcharge provisions and other special soil, subgrade, sub-base or base and surface compaction, or stabilization measures as may be required.
>
> 3. Draw up specifications supplementary to the Ministry's General Specifications for Highway Construction as may be necessary and

compose special provisions as required for the preparation of contract documents. Prepare bills of material, lists of drawings, explanatory material etc., as necessary to be included in the contract documents, and draw up separate lists and specifications of materials to be supplied by the Ministry and by others in respect to the contracts and to the project generally.

4. Prepare detailed quantity and cost estimates including engineering and contingency amounts, and costs of materials and services to be provided by the Ministry and by others to arrive at an accurate overall estimate of costs of the project, including estimated utility relocation costs but not including right of way costs.

The letter also contained this provision: "The Ministry will critically review the work as it proceeds and will advise on matters regarding policy as these are reached".

N D Lea carried out its assigned work, including the preparation of specifications and construction drawings. The construction drawings all bore the engineer's seal of one of N Walji, G Fary or W Reid, all professional engineers in the employment of N D Lea.

Design and tender documents incorporating the work of N D Lea & Associates were provided by the Ministry of Highways to prospective bidders in 1979. In October 1979 Edgeworth Construction Ltd ("Edgeworth") bid on 6.82 km of the project. By that time the work of N D Lea had been completed. In November 1979 a contract was awarded to Edgeworth to carry out the construction of those 6.82 km of the project. The contract documents included plans and specifications prepared by N D Lea. The plans bore the engineer's seals of Mr Walji, Mr Fary or Mr Reid. Functions were assigned to an "Engineer" under the contract. The "Engineer" was defined as the person holding the position or acting in the capacity of Assistant Deputy Minister Operations of Highways. N D Lea was not named in the contract and had no further function in relation to the contract.

The contract price was $6,985,245.35. Through extra work orders, unit price changes and other contract procedures, the actual amount paid to Edgeworth, in the end, was $19,444,249.64. Edgeworth has claimed a further $21,694,210.99. A large part of that claim is for interest on the principal amount actually paid under the contract in the end, and for interest on further amounts for which claims are made for work which may not have been covered by the contract terms.

II

Edgeworth began an action against N D Lea in September 1986

and an action against the individual engineers in October 1988. Statements of defence were filed in both actions. In October 1989 the defendants in both actions applied under Rule 18A, the summary trial rule, for judgments dismissing the two actions on the basis of two defences in each case; namely, first, that the actions were out of time under the Limitation Act, and second, that the defendants owed no duty in law to the plaintiff in the circumstances that I have described.

The second of those two questions was dealt with by the chambers judge on the basis that it involved no contested issue of fact, and that the allegations of fact in the statement of claim should be assumed to be true. On that basis it could also have been brought on for decision under Rule 34 on a point of law arising from the pleadings. The limitation question raises questions with a factual component about when a duty arose and when the plaintiff should have become aware of that duty. It was because those questions of fact were raised that the application was brought under Rule 18A.

For the purposes of the application, and on the basis of the pleadings, it was assumed that the design work for the project, including the preparation of the plans and specifications, was done carelessly; that the careless work was incorporated in the tender documents and in the contract documents; that Edgeworth relied on the tender documents and on the contract documents incorporating the careless work; and that the carrying out of the project on the basis of that reliance caused economic loss to Edgeworth. I emphasize that those were merely assumptions, made for the purpose of exposing the point of law. They have not been established by evidence.

Meredith J heard the application in Supreme Court chambers. He granted the application on the basis that there was no relevant duty of care in law on the part of N D Lea, or on the part of the individual engineers, to Edgeworth. Meredith J, having decided that there was no duty of care, did not deal with the limitation question.

This appeal is from Meredith J's decision. Counsel for Edgeworth said that the key question was whether N D Lea owed a duty of care, in law, in the circumstances, to Edgeworth. If there was no such duty, that was sufficient to dispose of the appeal. Only if there could be said to have been a duty owed by N D Lea to Edgeworth would it be necessary to consider the position of the individual engineers. So we were told, and we have considered this appeal on that basis.

III

This is a claim for negligent misstatement. The leading cases are *Hedley Byrne & Co* v *Heller & Partners Ltd* [1964] AC 456, in the

United Kingdom, and *Haig* v *Bamford* [1977] 1 SCR 466 [1976] 3 WWR 331, 72 DLR (3d) 68 in Canada. The most recent relevant authority of high significance is *Caparo Industries plc* v *Dickman* [1990] 2 WLR 358.

I do not think that it is desirable for me to undertake any detailed analysis of this field of law. Instead I propose only to state my conclusions about the present law as those conclusions affect the outcome of this appeal.

This cause of action depends on the existence of a duty of care. The duty arises from foreseeability, reliance, and proximity. It does not matter whether those three concepts are treated as aspects of each other or merely as being interrelated.

There must be foreseeability of economic loss being caused to someone in a specific class which is put at risk by the carelessness in question.

Reliance must be justifiable and reasonable and must be foreseeable by the person whose careless misrepresentation creates the risk.

The most elusive concept is proximity. It is the concept of proximity which has come to bear the heaviest burden in the decision-making process in this type of case. In the field of misrepresentation causing economic loss it means much more than physical connection. It encompasses all the circumstances that cause one person to depend in a reasonable way on another, and in such a way as to cause that other to bear the responsibility for carelessly created risks to the dependent person who is vulnerable to those risks.

In determining whether there is a relationship of sufficient proximity in a particular context where ample precedents have established the existence or non-existence of a duty of care, I think the proper course is to follow the precedents. In cases where there are no sufficient precedents, then I think the best course is to consider the individual circumstances very carefully rather than to apply one of the general theories of the law of negligence which have come and gone over the last few years. In reaching that conclusion I am adopting the view of Brennan J in *Sutherland Shire Council* v *Heyman* (1985) 60 ALR 1 at pages 43-44, 59 ALJR 564, which was endorsed by the Law Lords in *Caparo Industries plc* v *Dickman*. Of course such a consideration involves, in novel fact situations, an element of judgment. I prefer not to call that element of judgment a matter of policy and I prefer not to treat it as grafting a new "just and reasonable" test onto the law of negligence. Indeed, I consider that the House of Lords, which was responsible for the "just and reasonable" addendum, has now retreated from the "just and reasonable" test as an appropriate separate test: see *Caparo Industries plc* v *Dickman* and *Murphy* v *Brentwood District Council* [1990] 3 WLR 414; 50 BLR 1. In neither of those cases was a "just and reasonable" test applied. The "just and reasonable" test was not adopted by the majority of this court in *London Drugs Ltd* v *Kuehne & Nagel Int Ltd* 45 BCLR (2d) 1; [1990] 4 WWR 289; 70 DLR (4th) 51, but only by two out of five judges.

Instead, I think that the correct approach is to try to think of the particularly significant elements in the whole factual context of the case being considered and to try to draw parallels which are legally and practically meaningful between those elements and similar or comparable elements in cases where a duty of care has been found to exist or in cases where a duty of care has been found not to exist. That approach to the judgment function bears all the hallmarks of traditional legal reasoning. I propose to follow it, despite its defects, because other approaches based on a general theory of liability have proven to be less reliable and more unpredictable.

I do not think that the process of decision-making that I have described is helped by lists of the ingredients of this cause of action in terms of categories of one kind or another, framed in a general way, but moulded by the context of a specific case. So I do not propose to prepare or apply such a list.

IV

I know of no case in the Supreme Court of Canada, a provincial court of appeal, an Australian or New Zealand court of appeal or a United Kingdom court of appeal where an engineer or architect who did the design work for an owner under a contract with the owner was found liable to a contractor who suffered economic loss in the building of the work because of carelessness in the design work.

We were referred to three trial decisions of the High Court of Ontario which were said to support the view that such a liability may exist in law. Those three cases are *Brown & Huston Ltd* v *York* (1983) 5 CLR 240; *Cardinal Construction Ltd* v *Brockville* (1984) 4 CLR 149, 25 MP LR 116, and *Auto Concrete Curb Ltd* v *South Nation River Conservation Authority* (1988) 30 CLR 245.

In *Brown & Huston* and in *Auto Concrete Curb Ltd* the question of the liability of the engineer as an independent liability does not bear the hallmarks of having been thoroughly argued. And a good deal has happened in this area of the law since *Cardinal Construction Ltd* v *Brockville*. One of the important things that has happened is the decision of the English Court of Appeal in *Pacific Associates Inc* v *Baxter,* [1990] QB 993; 44 BLR 33 (CA), where an engineer who was assigned functions under a building contract and who was alleged to have carried those functions out carelessly was considered to have no duty of care to the contractor, independently of the duty of the owner under the contract.

The judgment in *Pacific Associates* v *Baxter* is notable in that it decided that the web of contractual relationship in a complex construction project formed a crucial element in the whole context which governed the determination of the question of proximity. That conclusion was adopted in several of the judgments of members of this court in *London Drugs* v *Kuehne & Nagel Int Ltd* and was not rejected in any of those judgments. I regard that point as a decisive factor in this case. It also throws new light on the proximity considerations underlying the three trial decisions in Ontario.

V

In this case Edgeworth Construction made a construction contract with the Crown, represented by the Ministry of Highways. The design of the project and the plans and specifications prepared by N D Lea were incorporated in the contract. They were adopted by the Ministry of Highways as the design, plans and specifications of the Ministry of Highways. They became representations of the Ministry of Highways to prospective bidders. When they were adopted and promulgated by the Ministry of Highways as the Ministry of Highways' representations they ceased to be the representations of N D Lea, at least insofar as proximity for the purposes of a duty of care with respect to economic loss is concerned. Proximity for the purposes of personal safety is a different matter, governed by different considerations. It is not in issue in this appeal. And, in my opinion, the individual seals of individual engineers make no difference in the context of this case to the question of proximity for the purposes of economic loss.

The contract dealt specifically with questions about what was to happen if the quantities were wrong or if extra work was required. The whole question of flaws in design or in the plans and specifications was an appropriate subject matter for the contract between Edgeworth Construction and the ministry. By contrast, N D Lea had no direct relationship with Edgeworth Construction. N D Lea's relationship was a contractual one with the ministry. N D Lea had no opportunity to define with Edgeworth Construction the risks that it was prepared to assume, if any, and the risks it was not prepared to assume, in relation to Edgeworth. N D Lea was not compensated on the basis that it would be assuming risks in relation to the prospective bidders and the final contractor. N D Lea could not control the contents of the contract between the ministry and Edgeworth. The ministry could have changed the design, the plans and the specifications before the tender documents were sent out or before the contract was made. N D Lea could not monitor whether the basis on which it did its work was precisely matched by the basis on which the construction contract was let. But, on the other hand, Edgeworth had an opportunity to protect itself in the contract with the Ministry of Highways in relation to the risks it was prepared to bear and the risks which it had to be protected against.

Having regard to the specific factors to which I have referred in the last two paragraphs, it is my opinion that there was no relationship of proximity between N D Lea on the one hand and Edgeworth on the other such as would support a duty of care on the part of N D Lea to Edgeworth to take all reasonable steps to avoid risk of economic loss by the successful bidder on the construction contract.

While a person can owe parallel and similar duties in contract and in tort, either both to the same person or one to one person and one to another, it is my opinion that in this case the contractual relationships were such that a tort duty should not be regarded as having been created on the part of N D Lea to Edgeworth in relation to economic loss arising from the performance of Edgeworth's contract with the Ministry of Highways.

VI

I would dismiss this appeal.

BADGERHILL PROPERTIES Ltd v BEVERLEY ANN COTTRELL and BEVERLEY ANN COTTRELL v BADGERHILL PROPERTIES Ltd and BRIAN TWIGG

8 May 1991 *Court of Appeal*

Mustill, Balcombe, and Woolf LJJ

Contract – Determining the parties – Trade names – Companies Act 1985, sec 36(4)

In 1986 the defendant wanted to have works done for a home for the elderly. She found an advertisement for "The Plumbing Centre". She telephoned and an appointment was made for a Mr Twigg to visit. When Mr Twigg visited he introduced himself as being from "The Plumbing Centre". No reference was made to the existence of a limited company. The defendant was subsequently provided with three estimates. Two, for the plumbing works, were signed by Mr Twigg as "Director" and headed "The Plumbing Centre" and had printed at the foot of the page "Registered Office: 215, Canterbury Street: Badgerhill Property Limited". The other estimate, for the building work, was in the same form except the trading name of Wendell (Builders) was printed at the heading and Mr Twigg was not described on the document as a director. After negotiations the defendant accepted the estimates in their final form.

In August 1987 the plaintiff issued a writ claiming £14,237 for work carried out by it for the defendant. The defendant counterclaimed for damages for alleged defects. Shortly before trial the defendant re-amended her counterclaim to allege that the contracts on which the counterclaim was based were made not between herself and the plaintiff company but between Mr Twigg and herself.

The defendant contended that she had not noticed the print at the bottom of the estimates and that as far as she was concerned Mr Twigg was doing the work under different names and had been the party with whom she had contracted. Alternatively the defendant relied upon section 36(4) of the Companies Act 1985 which provides,

> "Where a contract purports to be made by a company, or by a person as agent for a company, at a time when the company has not been formed, then subject to any agreement to the contrary the contract has the effect of one entered into by the person purporting to act for the company or as agent for it, and he is personally liable on the contract accordingly."

The trial judge rejected the defendant's alternative argument but held that the defendant had in fact contracted with Mr Twigg. Mr Twigg appealed.

***HELD**, allowing the appeal:*

(1) The contracts for the plumbing work were made in writing by the estimates as revised and signed by way of acceptance by the defendant. The question of the parties to the contracts was a matter of interpretation of the documents. The estimates suggested that the defendant was contracting with whoever was trading as "The Plumbing Centre". This was the plaintiff company whose name appeared on the notepaper (although misdescribed as Badgerhill Property), as suggested by the word "Director" underneath Mr Twigg's signature, and by the requirements of section 4 of the Business Names Act 1985 by which a company has to state its corporate name and address for service on all business letters.

(2) The contract for the building work had to be construed in the context of the series of contracts. When so construed, the absence of the word "Director" did not affect the analysis that the contract was made with whoever was conducting business under the name appearing at the top of the notepaper which was the plaintiff company.

(3) The misdescription of the company did not bring the facts within section 36(4) of the Companies Act 1985, since the contracts did not purport to be made by Badger Hill Property Ltd, but by whoever was using the trading names at the head of the notepaper. In fact, the company which was trading was Badgerhill Properties Ltd. *Oshkosh B'Gosh Inc.* v *Dan Martell Inc. Ltd.* [1989] BCLC 507 *followed.*

T Keith appeared on behalf of the appellant, instructed by Kingsley Smith and Co
Anthony Speaight appeared on behalf of the respondent, instructed by Girlings

Commentary

The issue about the contracting parties apparently arose only in consequence of doubts about the financial position of the plaintiff company. The defendant therefore changed tack and alleged that the contracts had been concluded between herself and Mr Twigg.

The relevant facts were not in dispute. This was not a case of ambiguity nor was it treated as such by the Court. The Court looked only at the documents themselves against the background of the relevant law, the Business Names Act 1985 and the Companies Act 1985. The distinction between "objective" and "subjective" facts in this context is sometimes not easy to draw. The defendant's evidence that she did not notice the printing on the bottom of the estimates was irrelevant. The defendant's evidence that she regarded the party with whom she contracted as being Mr Twigg was relevant, not to the issue of whether an agreement was reached with the plaintiff, but either to whether there was an intent to create legal relations with the plaintiff, or whether, if so, the contract so formed was void or voidable for mistake.

Considering only the objective facts in a sensible manner it is clear that the real question was: between whom were the three contracts made? (as Balcombe LJ said). Who therefore was using the trade name or names? Taking into account the admissible facts (principally, what was written on the face of the documents), was it the company described as Badgerhill Property Ltd? By a printing error, the company name was incorrectly printed, but it is clear from the judgments that the Court of Appeal was able to discard the difference in name, using only objective facts since it was plain that the trading name was being used by a company. A check upon the registered number would have revealed that the error was in the name. A search for Badgerhill Property Ltd would have revealed the non-existence of such a company. Not many customers of "The Plumbing Centre" would have done so, but this is also irrelevant. It was therefore obvious that Mr Twigg was not the contracting party but, as the contracts made clear, an agent on behalf of the company.

The Court of Appeal however agreed with the conclusion of the trial judge that section 36(4) of the Companies Act, 1985 did not help Mrs. Cottrell. The contract had in fact been made by a company: see *Oshkosh B'Gosh Inc* v *Dan Martell Inc Ltd* [1989] BCLC 507.

This appeal was an appeal against mixed findings of fact and holdings of law from a recorder sitting to hear Official Referees' Business. As noted in our commentary on *Hoskisson* v *Moody Homes Ltd* (1989) 46 BLR 81, the Rules of the Supreme Court now permit appeals from official referees generally on questions of fact, but subject to the leave of the official referee or of the Court of Appeal.

This case is an example of the type of case in which leave to appeal ought to be given. The points at issue were points of general importance for the law of contract and so the somewhat restrictive approach in the *Hoskisson* case ought not to be followed.

BADGERHILL PROPERTIES Ltd v BEVERLEY ANN COTTRELL and BEVERLEY ANN COTTRELL v BADGERHILL PROPERTIES Ltd and BRIAN TWIGG

8 May 1991 *Court of Appeal*

Mustill, Balcombe and Woolf LJJ

WOOLF LJ: This is an appeal by Mr Brian Twigg against a decision of Mr Recorder Havery QC when sitting to hear official referee's business on 16 March 1990. The decision of the recorder was as to a preliminary issue which had been ordered, by consent, to be tried between Mr Twigg and Mrs Beverley Ann Cottrell as to whether Mr Twigg could be personally liable on three contracts which had been entered into by Mrs Cottrell.

The order of 2 October 1989, which set out the issue which was to be determined, identified that issue by reference to paragraphs which had been introduced, by re-amendment, into Mrs Cottrell's defence and counterclaim on 28 April 1989. Prior to that amendment Mr Twigg had not been a party to the proceedings. Up to then the proceedings had been between Badgerhill Properties Ltd ("the company") and Mrs Cottrell. Those proceedings had been commenced by a writ issued by the company on 6 August 1987, endorsed with the statement of claim, in which the company claimed the sum of £14,327 in respect of work, services and materials sold and delivered by the company to Mrs Cottrell. By her defence and counterclaim, in its original form, Mrs Cottrell claimed a much greater sum, in excess of £80,000, including damages for loss of profit, arising out of the alleged defective way in which the work had been carried out by the company.

After the defence and counterclaim had been served it was discovered by Mrs Cottrell's advisers that the company was in financial difficulties and the proceedings were then re-amended so as to allege that the contracts, on which the counterclaim was based, were not made between the company and Mrs Cottrell, but between Mr Twigg, a director of the company, and Mrs Cottrell. The issue was to determine whether Mr Twigg could be personally liable to Mrs Cottrell as alleged in the re-amended defence and counterclaim.

In support of Mrs Cottrell's contention that Mr Twigg was personally liable, two separate arguments were advanced before the recorder.

The first argument was that Mr Twigg had contracted personally with Mrs Cottrell and had not contracted on behalf of the company. This argument was accepted by the recorder and his decision on this argument was sufficient to determine the issue in favour of Mrs Cottrell. However, the recorder also dealt with the second and alternative argument of Mrs Cottrell. This argument was that because the company's name was inaccurately set out in the letters which constituted the contract, Mr Twigg was personally liable as the result of the application of the provisions of section 36(4) of the Companies Act 1985. So far as this issue was concerned the recorder indicated that he would, if necessary, have decided this issue in Mr Twigg's favour.

The facts

Mrs Cottrell has business interests in hotels and rest homes for the elderly. In 1986 she purchased 15 Mansion Row, Brompton, Gillingham, Kent. She intended to have substantial works carried out at the premises with the intention of using them as a residential home for the elderly. The alterations to be carried out included building and plumbing works and the installation of central heating. Mrs Cottrell consulted the Yellow Pages in order to find someone to carry out the works. In the Yellow Pages, under the heading "Central Heating", there was a box advertising "The Plumbing Centre" at 160 Canterbury Street, Gillingham, and a telephone number. Under the heading "Plumbers", the Plumbing Centre was listed at *215* Canterbury Street, Gillingham, with the same telephone number. Neither entry made any reference to the existence of a limited company.

Early in November 1986, Mrs Cottrell telephoned the Plumbing Centre and inquired whether they could furnish her with an estimate for central heating and for plumbing at the Mansion House. An appointment was arranged for "their Mr Twigg to visit" 15 Mansion Row. "Mr Brian Twigg attended on behalf of the Plumbing Centre. He introduced himself as Mr Twigg from the Plumbing Centre." Mr Twigg asked Mrs Cottrell if she had arranged for anyone to carry out the building work. She said "No", and Mr Twigg then said "he had a building firm, named Wendell (Builders). It was arranged that Wendell (Builders) would give an estimate for carrying out the building work. Mr Twigg did not refer to any limited company at that meeting either with regard to the Plumbing Centre or Wendell (Builders)." (The above quotations are taken from Mrs Cottrell's proof of evidence which was treated as her evidence in chief at the hearing.)

As a result of Mr Twigg's visit Mrs Cottrell was provided with three estimates which were all dated 21 November 1986. Both the estimate for the central heating and the estimate for the plumbing work were on notepaper which was headed in large lettering "The Plumbing Centre". Beneath the heading was the address 215 Canterbury Street, Gillingham, Kent, and in smaller, but legible print at the foot of the page appeared the words "Registered Office: 215 Canterbury Street: Badgerhill Property Ltd". The estimate in describing the work frequently used the word "we" as opposed to "I". Both estimates concluded with the following words and were signed by Mr Twigg:

> "We trust this estimate meets with your approval and look forward to receiving your valued order.
>
> Yours faithfully,
> THE PLUMBING CENTRE
>
> B Twigg,
> Director."

Both estimates, under the heading, gave the same VAT number. That VAT number is the registered number, according to the certificate of registration for value added tax, of "Badgerhill Properties Ltd, T/A Plumbing Centre, 215 Canterbury Street". Badgerhill Propert*ties* Ltd is the correct description of the company which was incorporated on 7 December 1973, and the notepaper was in error in describing the company as Badgerhill Proper*ty* Ltd. The error was due to a mistake by the printer and had not been noticed by Mr Twigg.

The estimate for the building works was identical to the other estimates, except that it was on the notepaper of Wendell (Builders) and the word "Director" did not appear close to Mr Twigg's signature which appeared under "Wendell (Builders)". The same VAT number appeared. The same address appeared and, again, the company was misdescribed in the same way as "Badgerhill Property Ltd".

Negotiations followed. Both the plumbing and building estimates were revised and two revised estimates dated 26 January 1987 were provided for Mrs Cottrell. Having regard to the findings of the recorder, there is no relevant difference between the original estimates and the revised estimates. On 2 February 1987 Mrs Cottrell signed, by way of acceptance, and subsequently returned copies of the estimates in their final form.

Mrs Cottrell's evidence, which the recorder accepted, was that she made no distinction between the heating, plumbing and building contracts so far as the identity of the other contracting party was concerned. She said it was just Mr Twigg with several different firms. As far as she was concerned she was getting contracts for work and Mr Twigg did it under different names. She did not notice the reference to Badgerhill Property Ltd at the foot of the quotations.

These findings of the recorder have to be considered in the context of the limited evidence which Mrs Cottrell gave which included an answer which suggested that she was not really concerned as to who she was dealing with. This is consistent with what happened when the parties fell out and she was sued by the company, when Mrs Cottrell initially counterclaimed against the company, accepting that her contract had been with the company.

The first argument

Although there are allegations contained in the pleadings that there were collateral oral agreements and subsequent variations of the contracts, for the purposes of the preliminary issue, the case can be treated as involving three written contracts. The contracts were the estimates as revised, and the copies of the estimates which were signed by way of acceptance by Mrs Cottrell. In the first instance therefore the question of the possible personal liability of Mr Twigg depends upon the intention of the parties to be determined as a matter of interpretation of those documents considered against their "factual matrix". (See *Bowstead on Agency*, 15th Edn, Article 106 at page 445.)

On this approach, the situation appears clear; at least as to the two estimates on the Plumbing Centre notepaper. The notepaper sets out the trade name. The body of the estimates is couched in language which indicates that the estimate comes from the entity which is trading as the Plumbing Centre. The estimate ends by stating "Yours faithfully, THE PLUMBING CENTRE" and Mr Twigg's signature and name are followed by the word "Director". So far as those documents are concerned, their contents establish that Mrs Cottrell was accepting the estimates of the Plumbing Centre and that she was contracting with whoever was trading as the Plumbing Centre.

The fact that the company's name appeared on the notepaper (ignoring the misdescription for the moment) suggests that the Plumbing Centre was the trading name of the company. This suggestion is supported by the presence of the word "Director" below Mr Twigg's signature.

This suggestion is also supported by the fact that section 4 of the Business Names Act 1985 requires the company to state in legible characters on all business letters "its corporate name and an address in Great Britain at which service of any document relating to the business will be effective". The reference to the company, subject again to the error in the spelling, would appear to comply with this requirement.

So far as the third estimate from Wendell (Builders) is concerned, the position is not so strong so far as Mr Twigg is concerned because the word "Director" does not appear. However, the contract in relation to the building work has to be construed in the context of the series of contracts. Bearing in mind the similarities between the three contracts, I would not make any distinction based solely on the omission of the word "Director".

Here I obtain assistance from the judgment of Oliver LJ in *Phonogram Ltd* v *Lane* [1982] 1 QB 938. This was one of a number of cases to which we were referred which involved an agreement allegedly made on behalf of a not yet incorporated company. In relation to the position of those who sign a contrct on behalf of an unincorporated company Oliver LJ, at page 945, said:

> "Does the contract purport to be one which is directly between the supposed principal and the other party, or does it purport to be one between the agent himself — albeit acting for a supposed principal — and the other party? In other words, what you have to look at is whether the agent intended himself to be a party to the contract. So in *Kelner* v *Baxter* LR 2 CP 174 where the correspondence was directed to the agents and referred to 'the proposed company' which everybody knew was not yet in existence, there really was no room for the suggestion that the purchasers were acting in any other capacity than personally. On the other hand, in *Newborne* v *Sensolid (Great Britain) Ltd* [1954] 1 QB 45, where the contract was on the company's notepaper, it was clearly intended to be a company's contract (nobody realising that it had not yet been registered) and it could not be said that the individual plaintiff's signature in the company's name could possibly have been intended to make him a party to the contract.
>
> The case, in my judgment, does not rest on any narrow point as to the way in which the contract was actually signed. The result would have been exactly the same, in my judgment, as if the signature there had been accompanied by some such formula as 'for and on behalf of' or 'per pro'."

So here, I would regard each of the three contracts as being made between Mrs Cottrell and whoever was conducting business under the name appearing on the top of the notepaper, irrespective of the precise wording which appears next to the signature.

A trading name can of course be used by an individual, a partnership or a company. Here it is not suggested that Mr Twigg was conducting the business in partnership with the company or anyone else. Nor is it a case where it is suggested that Mr Twigg was jointly liable on the contracts with the company. The question is was he conducting the business of the Plumbing Centre? If he was, then whatever words he used in conjunction with his signature he would be liable. On the other hand, if business was being conducted by the company, then by signing as a director Mr Twigg would not incur personal liability. By signing he would be doing no more than signing the document in order to authenticate it as the document of the company which was using a trading name. The position would be similar to that in the case of *Newborne* v *Sensolid (Great Britain) Ltd* [1954] 1 QB 45 referred to in the passage already cited from the judgment of Lord Justice Oliver in *Phonogram Ltd* v *Lane*. In the *Newborne* case the complicating factor was that the company was not yet incorporated, whereas here the complicating factor was the use of the business name. In the *Newborne* case a distinction was drawn between the situation where a signature is applied to a document by way of authentication and the situation where a document is signed as the agent of a company by way of authentication of a company. This distinction can be a narrow one. It was explained in the judgment of Windeyer J in *Black* v *Smallwood* (1965-66) 117 CLR 52 in the High Court of Australia when he said in another case involving a not yet incorporated company the following:

> "If before the document sued upon was signed the registration of Western Suburbs Holdings Pty Limited had been completed and it had emerged from the Registrar General's office as a new-born entity in the law, no difficulty could have arisen. It could not then have been said that Smallwood and Cooper had contracted as agents on its behalf. It must have been said that it, not they, had made the contract. It, not they, would have been the purchaser entitled to a conveyance. Their putting the company's name to the document would have been purely in execution of its corporate act and their added signatures would have no more bound them personally to perform the contract than would the signatures of the directors or secretary of a company authenticating the affixing of its seal. There is a difference between a man's own acts and acts done for him by another man. The difficulty of the distinction in the case of a corporation is that a corporation must manifest its acts and intentions by the actions and declarations of human beings: and

> ambiguities and limitations of language make it difficult sometimes to express the distinction between acts done by a person as executant of the will of a corporation and acts done by a person as agent for a corporation, his principal. That the word 'agent' is in each case apt to describe the actor helps to disguise their different legal characters."

In his judgment, the recorder began correctly saying that, and I quote, "Mr Twigg purported to authenticate a contract entered into by The Plumbing Centre. By describing himself as a director, he indicated that The Plumbing Centre was, or was the business of, a limited company. In fact, The Plumbing Centre was merely a trading name and not itself a limited company. The argument put on behalf of Mr Twigg is that the legend at the bottom of the notepaper makes it clear that The Plumbing Centre is the trading name only of Badgerhill Properties Ltd, so that in effect any transaction entered into by The Plumbing Centre must be a transaction of that company." However, he then went on to add "if that was made clear, I would accept the argument that Mr Twigg would not be personally liable on that contract but in my judgment it was not. To adopt the words of Mellish LJ, which I have already quoted, the contractual documents in relation to the central heating contract do not contain anything 'very strong on the face of the instrument' to show that liability does not attach to Mr Twigg. I would reach that conclusion even if the company's name had been accurately stated in the legend. The misdescription only reinforces my conclusion."

The judgment of Mellish LJ to which the recorder referred was that in *Gadd* v *Houghton* (1876) 11 Ex D 357 at page 360. Mellish LJ in that case had emphasised that "when a man signs a contract in his own name, he is prima facie a contracting party and liable, and there must be something very strong on the face of the instrument to show that liability does not attach to him". This was said in the context of a situation where the issue was between the defendant being personally liable or not liable because he was an "agent" in the second sense that that word is used by Windeyer J. In *Gadd* v *Houghton* the test laid down by Mellish LJ was fulfilled by the words which appeared in the body of the text of the document "on account of". Here there were the references to the Plumbing Centre which made the position equally clear and once the recorder came to the conclusion that all that Mr Twigg was doing when he signed the document was to authenticate the contract entered into by the Plumbing Centre he was accepting that the terms of the contractual documents had fulfilled the requirement to which Mellish LJ referred. The contractual documents having made clear the capacity in which Mr Twigg signed, all that remained was to answer the separate question as to who was trading as the Plumbing Centre.

If the reference to the company on the notepaper was not sufficient to establish who was trading under the trading name, notwithstanding the fact that the address of the company given on the notepaper was the same as that given on the heading of the notepaper as being that of the business, then it was necessary to have regard to the other evidence which was available.

Unfortunately at the hearing the question was not properly explored. This was no doubt because it was only the day before the hearing that it was first suggested to Mr Twigg's legal advisers that Mrs Cottrell would suggest that Mr Twigg was personally liable under the contracts. However, what evidence there was all pointed one way. The certificate of registration for the purpose of VAT indicated that the company was trading as the Plumbing Centre. Mr Twigg was asked in cross-examination whether he "decided to do all the trading under the one company?". His answer was: "Correct". Mr Twigg also said that he had purchased the company "to trade under to limit my liability". Furthermore it was not even suggested by counsel appearing on behalf of Mrs Cottrell that Mr Twigg had in fact personally traded as the Plumbing Centre or as Wendell (Builders).

In those circumstances it was not open to the recorder to find that Mr Twigg was himself trading under those names which was an essential finding before he could be found personally liable once the recorder had come to the conclusion that Mr Twigg had merely authenticated the contract entered into by the Plumbing Centre.

I therefore come to a different conclusion to that of the recorder in relation to the first argument.

The second argument

My conclusion in relation to the first argument gives added significance to the second argument. This argument turns on the error which appears in the notepaper as to the name of the company. Mr Speaight submits that no company of the name Badgerhill Properties Ltd has been incorporated. He therefore submits he is entitled to rely on section 36(4) of the Companies Act 1985 which provided at the relevant time (it has since been amended) as follows:

> "Where a contract purports to be made by a company, or by a person as agent for a company, at a time when the company has not been formed, then subject to any agreement to the contrary the contract has effect as one entered into by the person purporting to act for the company or as agent for it, and he is personally liable on the contract accordingly."

The short answer to this argument, in my judgment, is that in this case the contracts did not purport to be made by Badgerhill Proper*ty* Ltd. They purported to be made by the Plumbing Centre and Wendell (Builders). For reasons already explained, Badgerhill Proper*ties* Ltd was the company which was carrying on business under those names and was therefore the party to the contract. The latter company had been "formed". The only relevance of the name Badgerhill Property Ltd appearing on the contractual documents was that it was an indication that the businesses were not being conducted by Mr Twigg personally but by a company and the name of that company was Badgerhill Property Ltd. It was therefore not a situation where Badgerhill Property Ltd had purported to make the contract.

However, quite apart from this simplistic approach, in *Oshkosh B'Gosh Inc* v *Dan Marbell Inc Ltd & Anr* [1989] BCLC 507 this court had to consider the effect of section 36(4) of the Companies Act 1985 which at the relevant time was contained in section 9(2) of the European Communities Act 1972. In *Oshkosh* it was argued that the section applies where a company has decided to change its name and has started trading under a new name but the certificate of incorporation under the new name has not yet been issued. The Court of Appeal took the view that although the company was at the material time acting and trading under an incorrect name it had been already duly formed by its incorporation. As Balcombe LJ indicated in the course of his judgment:

> "It seems to me that where the question is whether a contract purports to be made by a company, or a person as an agent for a company, it must be a matter of fact which is the company in question."

As to that issue of fact, there can be no doubt that the company which was trading and which entered the contract here was Badgerhill Properties Ltd and not Badgerhill Property Ltd. The former company had been incorporated so the section can have no application.

As to this argument the judgment of the recorder was correct.

It follows that I would allow this appeal. I would therefore determine the first issue by deciding that Brian Twigg cannot be personally liable to Mrs Cottrell as alleged in the relevant paragraphs of the re-amended defence and counterclaim.

BALCOMBE LJ: I have had the advantage of reading in draft the judgment of Woolf LJ. I agree with him and for the reasons which he gives that this appeal should be allowed, but as we are differing from the judge below I add a few words of my own.

The first issue on this appeal is: between whom were the three contracts made? There is no doubt that one party to all three contracts was Mrs Beverley Ann Cottrell. In two of the contracts the other party was whatever person or body was trading as "The Plumbing Centre"; in the third contract the other party was whatever person or body was trading as "Wendell (Builders)". On the facts as stated by Woolf LJ, it is clear that it was Badgerhill Properties Ltd that was trading as both "The Plumbing Centre" and "Wendell (Builders)". Mr Twigg's signature to the contracts did not mean that he was contracting as agent on behalf of the company; he was — to use the words of Windeyer J in *Black* v *Smallwood* (1965-66) 117 CLR 52 at page 61 — the executant of the will of the company to make the contracts and thereby manifesting the company's act of entering into the contracts. Accordingly I agree that it was with Badgerhill Properties Ltd that Mrs Cottrell made all three contracts.

On the second issue of the appeal I agree with the recorder and there is nothing which I can usefully add.

MUSTILL LJ: I agree with both the foregoing judgments and have nothing to add.

BLEXEN Ltd v G PERCY TRENTHAM Ltd

23 May 1990 *Court of Appeal*

Lloyd, McCowan LJJ
and Sir John Megaw

Arbitration – Sealed offer – Award for less than offer – Claimant not awarded full costs – Whether challenge to arbitrator's reasoned award on costs is by way of appeal or remission – Arbitration Act 1979 sec 1, Arbitration Act 1950 sec 22

Arbitration – Costs – Exercise of discretion where amendments after sealed offer.

The plaintiffs (Blexen) were sub-contractors to the defendants (Trentham). Disputes arose between them which were referred to arbitration. When pleadings in the arbitration closed in July 1986 Blexen claimed £221,000 and Trentham admitted only £7,000. On 4 August 1986 Trentham made a sealed offer to settle all claims in the arbitration for £77,000 (including interest). The offer was not accepted. In November 1986, just before the start of the hearing, Trentham amended its defence to plead that the rates in respect of dayworks should be assessed by reference to a different section of the FCEC Dayworks schedule to that used by Blexen. This defence was successful and reduced Blexen's claim by £34,000.

At the invitation of the parties the arbitrator made an interim award upon all issues save for costs. Blexen was awarded a sum which was £27,000 less than the amount of the sealed offer. On the issue of costs the arbitrator rejected Blexen's submission that it should be entitled to an award of costs since it contended that it had only failed to beat the sealed offer due to the amendment to the defence subsequent to the offer and that if it had known of the subsequent amendment at the date of the offer they would have accepted it. The arbitrator held that even if Blexen had known of the error in its dayworks claim it would still have rejected the sealed offer. He therefore awarded Blexen its costs only to the date of the offer but gave Trentham its costs thereafter.

Blexen applied pursuant to section 22 of the Arbitration Act 1950 for an order to remit the award of the arbitrator. Judge Lewis Hawser QC granted the order, holding that the arbitrator misconducted himself as he had applied the wrong test since he had treated the amendments as irrelevant whereas he should have asked whether Blexen had acted reasonably in continuing the arbitration after that date. Trentham appealed with leave, contending, inter alia, that a reasoned award on costs could only be challenged by appeal under section 1 of the Arbitration Act 1950.

***HELD** allowing the appeal:*

(1) The Court had no jurisdiction to remit the award to the arbitrator since an award of costs if wrong in law was capable of challenge only pursuant to section 1(3) of the Arbitration Act 1979.

(2) Even if it had jurisdiction, the court would not have remitted the award since there was no misconduct by the arbitrator who had taken the effect of the amendment into account in making his award and had found as a fact that Blexen would still have rejected the sealed offer even if the defence had been in its amended state at the date of the sealed offer.

John Dyson QC and John Rylance appeared for Trentham, instructed by Taylor Johnson Garrett
Anthony Thornton QC and Stephanie Barwise appeared for Blexen, instructed by Sandiford & Co, Bristol

Commentary
Prior to the Arbitration Act 1979 the power to remit under section 22 of the Arbitration Act 1950 was confined in respect of awards to errors appearing on the face of the award (or the reasons forming part of the award) except where it appeared that the arbitrator in his award had failed to exercise a discretion as to costs judicially. This case, however, makes it clear that in relation to errors in awards that power no longer exists. Where a reasoned award on costs is delivered the only right of challenge is that given by the Arbitration Act 1979. This case may be compared with the later case of *King* v *McKenna* at page 48 *below*, which concerned the power to remit in cases of "procedural mishaps".

In the *Blexen* case the arbitrator was addressed on all the issues concerning costs. He made findings of fact and rulings which Blexen did not accept. Had these findings of fact and rulings been made in the context of the substantive issues remitting in a reasoned award on these issues Blexen's only recourse would have been unquestionably limited to an application for leave to appeal pursuant to section 1 of the Arbitration Act 1979. Did it matter that the subject matter of the award which was challenged was the decision on costs? The Court of

Appeal held that it did not and that the form of procedure selected by Blexen was inappropriate. Whilst this in itself might not have been fatal to Blexen's application (since Blexen might still have got its case in order) Blexen's inability to find an error of law in the arbitrator's award clearly was.

King v *McKenna* shows whilst the true subject matter of the remedy of remission is not confined to "procedural mishaps" it clearly must have a procedural flavour. In the *Blexen* case that was no procedural mishap since the arbitrator was made aware of the sealed offer, was addressed upon the law and considered all the facts relevant to the issue of costs. As Lloyd LJ said, at page 42:

> "The arbitrator has explained his reasons for making his order as to costs in great detail in his final award. The award was made pursuant to an arbitration agreement. If the arbitrator had erred in his approach the error must be one of fact or law. If it was an error of fact his finding of fact is conclusive. If it was an error of law then it would be open to the claimants to apply for leave to appeal on that question of law. I can see no difference between an error of law in a reasoned award as to costs and any other error of law."

This decision and *King* v *McKenna* are best understood against the background of the structure of remedies which preceded the Arbitration Act 1979. The principal remedy for parties dissatisfied with the award of an arbitrator is now to be found by way of appeal under the 1979 Act. Even a complaint that there was no evidence upon which an arbitrator could have made an award is probably best regarded not as "misconduct" within section 23 of the 1950 Act or a matter raising an entitlement under section 22 of that Act but as a ground, albeit a weak ground, for an application for leave to appeal under the 1979 Act: see *Mustill and Boyd on Commercial Arbitration*, 2nd Edn at page 596.

Where the issue sought to be challenged is concerned with the question of costs only it is unlikely that leave to appeal will be given except in cases of plain disregard of established principle.

Practitioners will note that the court considered that where, as here, a late amendment had been allowed which substantially affected the claimant's prospects of success and which also resulted in the amount awarded being reduced below the sealed offer the proper approach was to consider whether the claimant would or would not have accepted the offer if the amendment had been made prior to the offer. This is consistent with the reverse case — where the claimant is permitted to amend so as to increase the claim — where the discretion as to costs must be exercised by reference to the case as originally pleaded: *Tingay* v *Harris* [1967] 2 QB 327; *Cheeseman* v *Bowaters Ltd* [1971] 1 WLR 1773.

BLEXEN Ltd v G PERCY TRENTHAM Ltd

23 May 1990 *Court of Appeal*

Lloyd, McCowan LJJ
and Sir John Megaw

LLOYD LJ: In this case we have been concerned with an order for costs made by an arbitrator, Mr D T Simmonds, after an arbitration lasting some fifteen days between November 1986 and January 1987. The facts, very briefly, are that the claimants, Blexen Ltd, were sub-contractors appointed by the main contractors, G Percy Trentham Ltd, to carry out certain works at the site of the former premises of the Imperial Metal Industries, Kynock, near Birmingham. The sub-contract works were carried out between July and November 1984. Disputes arose as to the amount due from the main contractors to the sub-contractors. Those disputes were referred to arbitration.

On 22 April 1986 the claimants served their points of claim, with schedules, in which they claimed that the amount owing was £221,000. On 13 June 1986 the respondents served their points of defence, consisting of nine short paragraphs and a schedule dealing with fifteen numbered items. They said that the total sum due under the sub-contract was £285,000, of which they had paid £278,000, leaving £7,000 due.

On 18 June 1986 the claimants served a very short reply and a schedule dealing with the same fifteen items. That was the state of the pleadings when, on 4 August 1986, the respondents made a sealed offer to settle all claims in the arbitration for the sum of £77,000 including interest to date. That offer was not accepted.

On 3 February 1987 the arbitrator made an interim award in which he awarded the claimants the sum of £52,958, including interest to the date of the award. The equivalent with interest to 4 August only, ie the date when the offer was made, was £49,867, so it was £27,000 less than the amount of the sealed offer.

There then followed a full day's hearing of the appropriate order for costs. The claimants claimed costs, saying that they were the successful party in the arbitration, having recovered an award of nearly £53,000. The respondents claimed costs on the grounds that the claimants had recovered less than they had been offered the previous August. The respondents therefore said that they should be regarded as the successful party. The claimants had failed to beat the sealed offer. The claimants replied that the respondents were only successful in that sense as a result of certain amendments to the defence subsequent to the offer. If the claimants had known of the subsequent amendments at the date of the offer they would have accepted it. In a reasoned award dated 19 October 1987 the arbitrator rejected the claimants' argument. He held that the claimants were entitled to their costs down to 7 August 1986, the date when they received the sealed offer, and that the respondents were entitled to their costs thereafter.

There was then an application by the claimants to remit the award to the arbitrator under section 22 of the Arbitration Act 1950. It came before His Honour Judge Hawser QC in the Official Referee's list on 30 May 1989. He held that the arbitrator had failed to apply the right test. I quote two paragraphs from his judgment:

> "(5) In my judgment if there are amendments made subsequently, the effect of which is to reduce the award below the offered figure, normally the court will deal with the question of costs on the basis of the situation as known to the plaintiffs at the time of the offer and not, as it subsequently transpired, by reason of the amendment. If on that basis the plaintiffs would have overtopped the offer normally they would be entitled to their costs at least up to the date of the amendments. Of course the arbitrator has a full discretion as to how far the amendments could properly be regarded as such, how much they amounted to, what effect they had on the arbitration and how far the arbitrator should properly be influenced by them. I do not think however that he can simply rule them out and treat them as being quite irrelevant, as I find he did here.
>
> (6) I do not think that the arbitrator considered the right question in this case. I accept that the correct question was whether the plaintiffs acted reasonably in continuing the arbitration after that date. If that question had been considered the answer might well have been different. In any event, the arbitrator should have considered the amendments and the effect which they would have in reducing the award to £49,000 instead of disregarding them entirely."

Accordingly, the learned official referee acceded to the plaintiffs' application. He remitted the award to the arbitrator on the grounds that the arbitrator had been guilty of technical misconduct.

There is now an appeal to this court. In giving leave, Lord Justice Bingham observed:

> "It seems to me doubtful whether a reasoned award on costs can be challenged on grounds of misdirection or legal error otherwise than by leave under section 1 of the 1979 Act."

We gave Mr Dyson, who appears on behalf of the respondents, leave to amend his notice of appeal so as to put that point in the very forefront of his case. I shall therefore deal with that point first.

Mr Thornton on behalf of the claimants produced for our assistance a helpful memorandum in which he traces the historical development of the court's power to interfere with an arbitrator's award as to costs. The basic rule has always been, at least since 1884, that the arbitrator has a complete discretion as to costs. See now section 18(1) of the 1950 Act. Originally the court could only intervene if it could be said that the arbitrator had exceeded his jurisdiction in making his award as to costs. As a result of an amendment to what is now section 22 of the 1950 Act, introduced by section 15 of the 1934 Act, it was more often put on the basis of technical misconduct. Nowadays, the question has to be considered in the light of section 1 of the 1979 Act. That section provides that the court shall not have jurisdiction to set aside or remit an award on an arbitration agreement on the grounds of errors of fact or law on the face of the award.

Mr Thornton argues that the wrongful exercise of the arbitrator's discretion as to costs does not give rise to any question of law. If it does, it is not a question of law arising out of an award on an arbitration agreement within the meaning of section 1(2) of the 1979 Act and therefore section 1(1) does not apply.

I find that argument difficult to follow. The arbitrator has explained his reasons for making his order as to costs in great detail in his final award. The award was made pursuant to an arbitration agreement. If the arbitrator has erred in his approach the error must be one of fact or law. If it was an error of fact his finding of fact is conclusive. If it was an error of law then it would be open to the claimants to apply for leave to appeal on that question of law. I can see no difference between an error of law in a reasoned award as to costs and any other error of law.

Then it was said that even if there was an error of law on the face of the award there is a parallel jurisdiction to set aside or remit for misconduct which survives the 1979 Act. The claimants can therefore choose their remedy. I do not agree. It is of course perfectly true that Parliament did not in 1979 repeal section 23 of the 1950 Act. The power to set aside or remit for misconduct survives. But the question is whether that power exists when the only misconduct alleged is an error of fact or law in a reasoned award. I am quite clear that it does not. To hold otherwise would defeat one of the main purposes of the 1979 Act. Whatever may have been the position as to costs in the old days, the only course open today, where an arbitrator states his reasons, is to challenge those reasons by seeking leave to appeal on a question of law under section 1(3) of the 1979 Act. This the claimants never did.

I say nothing about what would be the appropriate procedure when an arbitrator states no reasons for his award as to costs.

On the short ground that the judge had no jurisdiction to remit this award to the arbitrator, I would allow this appeal.

But it is right that we should go on to deal with the question of substance, not least because, as the judgment stands, the arbitrator has been found guilty of misconduct. He is entitled to have our views on that question, a question which has in any event been fully argued.

In his final award on costs the arbitrator set out the arguments on each side as he understood them. He rejected the respondents' argument that the claimants should be deprived of their costs on the ground that their claim was grossly exaggerated. He rejected their argument on the grounds that the claimants had failed on a number of discrete issues. That left only the respondents' offer of 4 August 1986 which was, as we have seen, for more than the claimants ultimately recovered. On the face of it that would entitle the respondents to their costs thereafter. But the claimants had an answer, namely, to rely on the subsequent "amendments" to the defence, which had, they say, the effect of reducing the amount which they ultimately recovered.

The principal amendment relied upon related to the rates chargeable for dayworks. Throughout the currency of the contract the claimants had submitted, and the respondents had paid, invoices for plant based on rates set out in schedule 3 of the Federation of Civil Engineering Contractors schedules of dayworks. It was only on 20 or 21 November 1986, just before the arbitration started, that the respondents realised that they ought to have been charged on a different basis, namely, that set out in paragraph 3 of schedule 4. The difference amounted to £19,788 in the respondents' favour. In his interim award the arbitrator found it extraordinary that the error had been allowed to pass unnoticed for so long. But he went on to say that he did not consider that that failure by all concerned (which would, of course, include the claimants) to detect the error, thereby created an agreement to supersede the contract conditions and use the claimants' claimed plant rates instead.

The arbitrator returned to the same point in his final award. Rightly or wrongly he seems to have understood the claimants to have been submitting that they, the claimants, were entitled to the costs, or at any rate were not liable for the costs, because the contract had been amended by the conduct of the parties. The arbitrator rejected that argument. It is not suggested that he was wrong to have done so, or that in doing so he misconducted himself in any way. If he misunderstood the claimants' submission, which I would not suppose that he had done, but if he did, and if he confused amendment of the contract with amendment of the defendants' points of defence, then that misunderstanding and that confusion was entirely immaterial.

As for the amendment to the points of defence, the argument, as the arbitrator understood it, was that if the claimants had known of the subsequent amendment at the time of the offer, it would have put the offer "in an entirely different light": see page 9 of the final award on costs. At page 13 the arbitrator records the claimants as having argued that the offer would, in those circumstances, have been accepted. Mr Thornton contended that no such argument was ever in fact advanced. It is nowhere reflected in Mr Keary's affidavit. But that submission I find hard to reconcile with the clear finding by the arbitrator as to the way that the case was put by Mr Neville in oral submissions on behalf of the claimants. And I note that in paragraph 38 of Mr Neville's affidavit he says that he had always been well aware that the claimants would have accepted £77,000 if they had known at the time of the offer of the subsequent amendment. So it would not have been surprising if Mr Neville had advanced that as an argument at the hearing before the arbitrator.

How then did the arbitrator deal with that argument? I quote three paragraphs from page 13 of the final award, as follows:

> "I have come to the conclusion that Mr Keary would still have rejected the offer. The Claimant's contention was that its own 'schedule' of Daywork Rates (as used during the currency of the Contract) was the correct one not the FCEC Schedule so it would not have mattered which Section of the latter the Respondent had elected to use in its calculations, it would still have been wrong in the eyes of Mr Keary.
>
> If the Claimant had priced its Dayworks in accordance with the FCEC Schedule Section 4 its total daywork claim (Items 14-J) would have been some £34,000 less reducing the overall claim from £210,420 to £186,246 and I do not think such reduction would have affected Mr Keary's decision to reject the offer of £77,000. Clearly the Claimant had high expectations of obtaining substantial amounts against the other items of the Claim, and it was, I consider, the overall prospect which governed Mr Keary's decision to reject rather than an anticipated award with respect to any one item.
>
> I conclude therefore that knowledge at 4th August 1986 of the subsequent amendment to the Defence as regards Daywork Items 14-J would not have resulted in the Claimant coming to a different decision in considering the Respondent's offer than it did."

That is, as I read it, a clear finding of fact that the subsequent amendments made no difference. The claimants would have rejected the offer in any event even if the defence had already been amended when the offer was made. I do not see how, in the light of those three paragraphs, it could be correct to say, as the judge said, that the arbitrator had disregarded the amendments altogether. He did not disregard the amendments. He took account of the amendments, but held that they would not have affected the claimants' decision to go ahead.

Then it was said, in the passage I have quoted from the judge's judgment, that the arbitrator asked himself the wrong question. He should have asked himself whether the claimants acted reasonably in deciding to go ahead with the arbitration after they had received the respondents' offer. But as I read the final award, that is precisely the question which the arbitrator did ask himself. At the foot of page 11 he says:

> "There remains the question, was the Claimant justified in refusing the offer on the material it had at the time?"

By inference he answered that question in the negative. The arbitrator cannot fairly be criticised if, in the course of answering that question, he dealt with the further question whether the claimants would have accepted the offer if they had known of the subsequent amendments, when that was the very question which the claimants themselves asked the arbitrator to consider.

So, with great respect to the judge, I can find no shadow of misconduct on the part of the arbitrator in the way he dealt with costs, not even misconduct of the most technical kind. So, even if we had jurisdiction to remit this award on grounds of misconduct, which we have not, I would have declined to exercise that jurisdiction on the facts of the present case. That being so, it becomes unnecessary to deal with the further question, which logically comes first, whether there was in truth any relevant amendment to the pleadings at all.

Mr Thornton relies on various references to "the amended pleadings" in the arbitrator's final award. But what do such references amount to? The claimants' various daywork claims were included in items 14 and 15. In the schedule to the points of defence the respondents say, with regard to both those items, that they required further information before commenting on them. So, on the pleadings as they stood at the time of the respondents' offer, the respondents were putting forward no positive case at all on the daywork items. They were holding their fire. The fact that the respondents had not challenged the basis on which the claimants had submitted invoices during the currency of the contract, and had indeed themselves submitted invoices under the head contract on the same basis, is wholly irrelevant. Once the parties were in dispute the respondents were fully entitled to put the claimants to proof of their claim. This is what they did. I do not see how they could have made it clearer than they did in their defence that the daywork items were in issue. When, therefore, the arbitrator refers to the amended pleadings he must, I think, have been referring to the particulars which were only furnished for the first time on 21 October, and subsequently revised on 17 November and 2 December. Such revised particulars would not have required any amendment to the points of defence. They were doing no more than filling in a gap in the original schedule, a gap which had necessarily been left open until further particulars had been furnished by the claimants.

Mr Thornton argued that strictly the respondents ought to have reduced the sum of £285,000 for which they accepted liability in paragraph 3 of the points of defence, but that would hardly have been the sort of amendment which would have justified the arbitrator in departing from the ordinary rule as to costs where there has been a sealed offer or payment into court. So Mr Dyson was right when he submitted that, so far as dayworks were concerned, there never was any relevant amendment to the defence as it stood at the time of the offer.

The same is also true (perhaps more true) of the two payments by the respondents amounting to £11,600, which it was agreed at a very late stage should be credited against the claimants' claim. I regret that I was quite unable to understand how that involved any amendment at all to any pleading, not even to the figure of £278,000 in paragraph 3 of the points of defence, since it was accepted by Mr Thornton, as I understood him, that the £11,600 was included in that figure. I need not mention the third amendment, which had the effect of reducing the amount awarded by only about £5,000.

At the conclusion of his argument Mr Thornton invited us to consider giving him leave to appeal on a question of law under section 1(3) of the 1979 Act, should we be against him on the jurisdiction question but in his favour on the point of substance. Ordinarily such an application for leave would have had to be made to the High Court, not to us. But since I am against him on both points the question does not arise.

Finally I should return to the point canvassed by the judge, namely, what was the correct question for the arbitrator to have asked himself. I do not find it possible to answer that question in a way which will provide much, or perhaps any, useful guidance for the future. The only case in which a similar question has been considered by this court was the case of *Cheeseman* v *Bowaters*

United Kingdom Paper Mills Ltd [1971] 1 WLR 1773. That was a personal injury case in which the plaintiff recovered £749 on the case as pleaded at the commencement of the trial. There was then a sum of £750 in court. In the course of the trial the plaintiff amended to plead a completely new case, as a result of which he recovered more than the sum in court. It was held by the Court of Appeal, reversing the judge, that the defendants ought to have their costs subsequent to the payment in.

It is not easy to apply that principle directly when it is the defendant who amends to plead a new defence rather than a plaintiff who amends to plead a new claim. But Mr Dyson conceded, correctly in my judgment, that the general rule should apply where the defendant amends to plead a new defence on which the burden rests on him, for example, a plea of limitation for liability or of some relevant contractual exception. In such a case, if the effect of the amendment is to reduce what would otherwise have been awarded below the sum paid in, it would usually be just to give the plaintiff his costs. In addition, it is normally preferable for the judge or an arbitrator to consider what would have been the result but for the amendment, rather than the simple question whether the plaintiff acted reasonably in continuing with the arbitration or the action on the pleadings as they stood, or the more elusive question, whether the plaintiff would or would not have accepted the offer, had he known of the future amendments.

Further than that I do not find it necessary or desirable to go. Each case, as is so often said, must be considered in the light of its own particular facts. Where an unfettered discretion has been granted by Parliament it is never desirable to hedge it about with too much guidance, in case the guidance comes to be regarded as an inflexible rule of law or practice. It can be no such thing.

For the reasons given earlier I would allow this appeal and quash the order for remission. The arbitrator's award as to costs will stand.

McCOWAN LJ: I agree.

SIR JOHN MEGAW: I also agree.

M F KING trading as ROBINSONS GARAGE M F KING HOLDINGS (UK) Ltd v THOMAS McKENNA Ltd and HOLBEACH PLANT HIRE Ltd

20 December 1990 *Court of Appeal*

Lord Donaldson MR,
Ralph Gibson and Nicholls LJJ

Arbitration – Award – Existence of sealed offer not brought to attention of arbitrator before award – Award unjust – Remission – Arbitration Act 1950, section 22 – Grounds for the exercise of discretion – Sealed offer

The plaintiffs were employers of the defendant civil engineering contractors. The contractors commenced an arbitration in which they claimed £25,000 and the employer counterclaimed £5,000. The arbitration was protracted and costly. The employer made a sealed offer to pay £5,000 in settlement of all issues in the arbitration. At the conclusion of the hearing, as a tactical decision, counsel for the employers mistakenly did not invite the arbitrator to make an interim award dealing with all issues except costs but instead asked for the issue of costs to be "held over" nor was a copy of the sealed offer given to him with instructions that it was to be opened by him after he had determined all issues save costs. Counsel was, however, mistaken in thinking that she had achieved her object. Accordingly, the arbitrator was unaware of the existence of the sealed offer or of any need to make an award which did not deal with costs. The arbitrator set off the amount which he would have awarded on the counterclaim against the amount he awarded on the claim and made an award of the balance in favour of the contractors in the sum of £4,743.51 and awarded the costs of the arbitration to the contractors.

By an originating summons the employer applied pursuant to section 22 of the Arbitration Act 1950 for an order remitting the award to the arbitrator so that he could reconsider his order as to costs in the light of the sealed offer. Hobhouse J ordered that the award should be remitted. The contractors appealed.

The Court of Appeal heard the appeal consecutively to the appeal in *Indian Oil Corporation Ltd* v *Coastal Bermuda Ltd* (from a decision of Evans J reported at [1990] 2 Lloyd's Rep 407, "the *Indian Oil* appeal"). In that appeal it was argued that the court had no jurisdiction to remit an award except in limited circumstances. In the *King* appeal it was common ground that there were no such strict limitations. Before judgment the *Indian Oil* appeal was compromised.

HELD *dismissing the appeal:*

(1) The issue of the scope of section 22 had been argued in the *Indian Oil* appeal and even though the point had not been argued in the *King* case the court had to decide it since it went to jurisdiction.

(2) Under section 22 of the Arbitration Act the jurisdiction to remit was unlimited. The exercise of that jurisdiction by the court would be exercised not by reference to traditional grounds for remission but because there had been some mishap or misunderstanding so that the case was not properly adjudicated for whatever reason. Since counsel's error was a mistaken belief that she had made a request for an interim award, which might be called a "mishap", it would be inequitable to give effect to the award without further consideration by the arbitrator.

per Lord Donaldson, MR:

"In my judgment the remission jurisdiction extends beyond the four traditional grounds to any cases where, notwithstanding that the arbitrators have acted with complete propriety, due to mishap or misunderstanding, some aspect of the dispute which has been the subject of the reference has not been considered and adjudicated upon as fully or in a manner which the parties were entitled to expect *and* it would be inequitable to allow any award to take effect without some further consideration by the arbitrator. In so expressing myself I am not seeking to define or limit the jurisdiction or the way in which it should be exercised in particular cases, subject to the vital qualification that it is designed to remedy deviations from the route which the reference should have taken towards its destination (the award) and *not* to remedy a situation in which, despite having followed an unimpeachable route, the arbitrators have made errors of fact or law and, as a result, have reached a destination which was not that which the court would have reached."

Richard Fernyhough QC appeared for the appellant contractor, instructed by Hawkins, Kings Lynn.
David Gardam QC and Simon Lofthouse (neither of whom appeared in the arbitration) appeared for the respondent building owners, instructed by Greenwoods, Peterborough

Commentary
The case is concerned with a "misunderstanding or mishap" in relation to a sealed offer. The purpose of sealed offers is well known. No machinery exists in arbitration which is equivalent to that provided by RSC Order 22 which enables a party to make a payment into court as an offer to settle the case against him. Thus the practice has developed of written offers being made on a without prejudice basis save as to costs. If the offer is not accepted within the time specified it is placed in a sealed envelope and given to the arbitrator to be read after he has reached his decision on all issues other than costs with a view to the arbitrator then exercising judicially his discretion as to costs in the same way as a judge would in relation to a payment in. Thus, unless there are special circumstances, a party who fails to recover more than the amount offered (questions of subsequent interest aside) will ordinarily recover costs only up to the date of the offer, will not recover any costs incurred thereafter and will instead have to pay the other party's costs since they would not have been incurred had the offer been accepted. Sealed offers are therefore like *Calderbank* letters (see *Cutts* v *Head* [1984] 1 All ER 597 and the limitations on the procedure exemplified by *Corby DC* v *Holst* (1984) 28 BLR 35.

Because of fears (based alas on a few exceptional but salutary instances) that an arbitrator might be influenced either by knowledge of the very existence of the award or might inadvertently or otherwise open the envelope and read the offer before completing the award and also because in complicated arbitrations where, whatever the outcome, there may be arguments as to costs, it is now the recognised practice that where a sealed offer has been made an arbitrator, will be asked by the party likely to be affected by it to make an interim award as to all issues save as to costs. As Lord Donaldson MR observed at page 63 *below*, an arbitrator who is invited to proceed in this way should accept the invitation and should not read anything into it since it might be made for a number of reasons not including the fact that an offer has been made. Some make the request for an interim award both at the outset of the arbitration and also in writing (in much the same way in which an arbitrator is asked to give a reasoned award) so as to avoid the possibility that the request is overlooked at the conclusion of the hearing and to avoid any misunderstanding. It would therefore be misconduct for an arbitrator not to accede to such a request. The procedure is close to that adopted in the High Court when the question of costs is dealt with at the conclusion of the judgment.

An alternative method of dealing with a sealed offer is to present the arbitrator before the conclusion of the hearing with a sealed envelope in which the offer is contained with instructions that the envelope is not to be opened until all matters save costs have been determined. (Even where no offer has been made parties using this method sometimes give the arbitrator a sealed envelope containing a statement to that effect. In these circumstances, this procedure appears to be rather solemn mummery designed to keep the arbitrator guessing.) This approach is appropriate only when the determination of the issues in the case is likely to lead to a simple monetary award one way or another and where the possibility of a complicated provision for costs is not sufficiently significant to justify the costs of further submissions to the arbitrator and a further award of costs.

In *King*'s case, as a result of what Hobhouse J held to be a mistake by counsel no sealed envelope was given to the arbitrator and nor was he invited to make an interim award. Unsurprisingly, the arbitrator awarded the costs to the contractor. The dilemma for the court was that the arbitrator's award of costs was the right award in the circumstances known to the arbitrator without fault on his part or on the part of the contractor. Should the court follow a policy of non-interference with arbitration or should it set right what was, taking into account all the circumstances, an obvious wrong? Solely as a result of the mistake the contractors got a windfall award on costs which was quite unjustified as they had been offered more than the amount awarded and ought therefore to have been penalised on costs.

In the *Indian Oil* case, Evans J did not regard these principles as conflicting, for he said at [1990] 2 Lloyd's Rep 407, at page 414:

> "According to *Russell on Arbitration* 19th and 20th Edns):
>
> > '... there is a never-ending war between two irreconcilable principles, the high principle which demands justice though the heavens fall, and the low principle which demands that there should be an end to litigation.'
>
> I must admit that I do not read the authorities in this way. True, the power should not be exercised unless the failure to do so would or might cause injustice to the applicant: compare *The Aros* [1978] 1 Lloyd's Rep 456 at page 463 *per* Brandon J. But at the same time it is of 'over-riding importance' that the finality of awards shall be preserved which, on any view of the matter, imposes severe restraints on the exercise of the statutory power: *per* Sir Roger Ormrod in *The Montan* [1985] 1 Lloyd's Rep 189 at page 198.

> These two factors, in my view, are not inconsistent with each other. If either of them is to prevail, then it should be the requirement of justice. But justice, even fairness, is not an abstract concept. It has to be applied in this context between two parties who were in dispute with each other and who agreed that the dispute should be resolved by an arbitral tribunal. They agreed that the tribunal's award should be final. But they agreed this on the basis that the arbitration procedures would be regulated by law. The court has statutory power to set aside an award when the arbitrators misconduct themselves or the reference — section 23 of the 1950 Act — but it also has the unqualified discretion to remit the award to the chosen tribunal under section 22. If the power is exercised, but only in circumstances when it would be unjust not to do so, then there is not, in my judgment, an uncovenanted nor an unacceptable restriction on the agreed finality of the tribunal's award. As Lord Atkin said in a different context, recently cited with approval by the Court of Appeal (Criminal Division): 'Finality is a good thing, but justice is better'. (*Ras Behari Lal* v *The King-Emperor* (1933) 50 TLR 1)."

The Court of Appeal resolved this conflict by a different approach. Since the State has the monopoly of coercion (as Lord Donaldson expressed it, it is "the ultimate enforcer" of the award) it had a responsibility not to ensure that the award was the *right* award, but to ensure that the award, (whatever it was), was arrived at by the right route, even where the responsibility for the deviation from the right route was that of a party seeking the remission.

The approach of Lord Donaldson has the virtue of simplicity, see page 60:

> "Whilst it may be impossible, or at least undesirable, to seek to determine these limits, save on a case by case basis, I personally find it helpful to ask myself what in truth the parties accepted when they agreed to arbitrate, although I am far from saying that this is the exclusive touchstone."

Nevertheless, the Court of Appeal in holding that the power to remit is not limited (as had previously been thought) has caused consternation amongst some practitioners. It can easily be seen how advantage might be taken of what is subsequently meant to appear as a mishap or misunderstanding, perhaps brought about by a supposed mistake by a party's lawyer. Thus, a party who has lost might dismiss his lawyer and instruct new lawyers with a view to having the award remitted on the grounds that the previous lawyer had made mistakes which resulted in an inadequate result. The approach appears also to run contrary to the supposed philosophy of the Arbitration Act 1979 — see for example *Blexen*'s case above at page 37. Perhaps the position will be clarified in any new arbitration legislation.

An important qualification made by Lord Donaldson MR was,

however, emphasised by Ralph Gibson LJ, namely that if the failure to put the sealed offer before the arbitrator at the appropriate time had been a deliberate tactical choice by the building owner or his lawyer then the court would not have intervened:

> "The making of a considered decision not to secure an opportunity for consideration by the arbitrator of the sealed offer by asking for the issue of costs to be stood over can, therefore, be ruled out with a sufficient degree of certainty to justify the order of remission. I regard that as important because the jurisdiction to remit should not, in my judgment, be available to enable a party to an arbitration to repent a considered decision by himself or his legal representatives with reference to such a matter in order for how to pursue a different course on remission to the arbitrator."

In this case on the facts found there was a deliberate tactical decision not to use the sealed envelope route but to ask that the issue of costs should be stood over; the lack of clarity with which this tactical decision was implemented was inadvertent, not deliberate.

M F KING trading as ROBINSONS GARAGE M F KING HOLDINGS (UK) Ltd v THOMAS McKENNA Ltd and HOLBEACH PLANT HIRE Ltd

20 December 1990 *Court of Appeal*

Lord Donaldson MR,
Ralph Gibson and Nicholls LJJ

LORD DONALDSON MR: We were asked by the parties to this appeal to hear it together with, or at least consecutively to, another appeal, *Indian Oil Corporation Ltd* v *Coastal Bermuda Ltd,* 'the Indian Oil Appeal". This was arranged and with the assistance of counsel appearing in the Indian Oil Appeal, which was the first to be heard, we explored the general background to the power of the court to remit arbitration awards pursuant to section 22 of the Arbitration Act 1950. There was then an interval before we heard argument in this appeal.

After the argument in both appeals had been concluded and we were on the brink of handing down our judgments, we were told that the parties to the Indian Oil Appeal had composed their differences. This was in many ways welcome news, but it has created a problem.

In the Indian Oil Appeal it was contended strongly that the jurisdiction to remit an award under section 22 was very limited. By contrast in *M F King Holdings Ltd* v *Thomas McKenna Ltd* ('this appeal") it was common ground that there was no such strict limitation. But for the settlement, we should have delivered a combined judgment disposing of both appeals In the first part, which would have dealt with the Indian Oil Appeal, we should have considered the general scope of the jurisdiction and then applied the law as we found it to the situation disclosed in that appeal. In the second part of the judgment, which would have dealt with this appeal, we would have considered the additional submissions on the law which were made in this appeal and applied them to the facts of this appeal.

This combined judgment was in an advanced state of preparation when we learnt of the settlement. In the changed circumstances it would clearly be inappropriate for us to express any conclusions which we have reached as to the rights of the parties to the Indian Oil Appeal. However, in fairness to the arbitrators in that case, we wish to make it clear that we would not have upheld the finding of any element of "mishandling" or "technical misconduct" on their part.

This leaves the argument that the scope of section 22 is very limited. If this had not gone to jurisdiction, it would have sufficed to say that neither party in this appeal wished to take the point. However, once serious doubt had been cast upon the width of our jurisdiction in a context which could have affected this appeal, albeit it was only raised in the other appeal, it became our duty to consider and rule upon it. I therefore propose first to consider the jurisdictional arguments canvassed in the Indian Oil Appeal, so far as they are of general application and relevant to this appeal, and then consider the arguments specifically referable to this appeal.

The scope of the power to remit

Prior to the passing of the Common Law Procedure Act 1854, control over arbitrations by the High Court was largely undertaken by the use of writs of *certiorari.* Apart altogether from the technicalities which surrounded the use of this remedy, it had the undoubted disadvantage that it was an "all or nothing" remedy. The court either quashed the award and sent the parties back to square one or it did nothing. The only exception was where the parties had incorporated a "Richards' clause" in the arbitration agreement. This clause, whose author was "Mr Richards, the average stater", gave the High Court consensual authority to remit the matters in question, or any of them, to the arbitrators instead of setting the whole award aside. One hundred and fifty years later the Richards family are still prominent in the profession of average stating, or "average adjusting" as it is now known, Mr William Richards having been chairman of the Average Adjusters' Association in 1983 and my own deputy chairman in 1982.

The legislative history of section 22 of the 1950 Act is as follows. Basing itself upon Mr Richards' clause, Parliament provided in section 8 of the Common Law procedure Act 1854, that:

> "In any case where reference shall be made to arbitration as aforesaid the Court or a Judge shall have power at any time, and from time to time, to remit the matters referred, or any or either of them, to the reconsideration and re-determination of the said arbitrator, upon such

> terms, as to costs and otherwise, as to the said Court or Judge may seem proper."

Parliament also provided in section 5 that an arbitrator could, if he thought fit and if the arbitration agreement did not otherwise provide, state his award or any part of it in the form of a special case for the opinion of the court.

The Arbitration Act 1889, re-enacted the substance of these sections as follows:

> "10(1) In all cases of reference to arbitration the Court or judge may from time to time remit the matters referred or any of them, to the reconsideration of the arbitrators or umpires.
>
> 19. Any referee, arbitrator or umpire may at any stage of the proceedings under a reference, and shall, if so directed by the court or a judge, state in the form of a special case for the opinion of the Court any question of law arising in the course of the reference."

Section 10 of the 1889 Act has survived virtually unchanged as section 22 of the Arbitration Act 1950, which reads:

> "22. *Power to remit award.* (1) In all cases of reference to arbitration the High Court or a judge thereof may from time to time remit the matters referred, or any of them, to the reconsideration of the arbitrator or umpire."

The substance of section 19 in a more elaborate form survived as section 9 of the Arbitration Act 1934 and as section 21 of the 1950 Act until that section was repealed by section 8(3)(b) of the Arbitration Act 1979.

The first, and most fundamental, of the submissions made in the Indian Oil Appeal was that section 22 did not authorise the court to remit an award to arbitrators for reconsideration on any ground except such as before the passing of the Common Law Procedure Act 1854 would have induced it to set the award aside or to treat it as a nullity in an action brought upon it. These grounds were (1) where the award was bad on its face, (2) where there had been misconduct on the part of the arbitrator, (3) where there had been an admitted mistake and the arbitrator had asked that the matter be remitted and (4) where additional evidence had been discovered after the making of the award.

This submission is somewhat startling in the light of the plain words of the section, but it is not unsupported by authority (see, for example, *Mills* v *The Society of Bowyers* (1856) 3 K & J, *Hodkinson* v *Fernie* (1857) 3 CB (NS) 189 and *Hodge* v *Burgess* (1858) 3 H & N

293). Indeed the learned editors of *Mustill & Boyd on Commercial Arbitration* (2nd Edn, 1989 at page 550) take the view that the weight of authority supports this view, at least if one adds two categories relating to the statement of a special case, which are no longer relevant, and a category which they describe as "a misunderstanding leading to injustice, even though the arbitrator has not committed misconduct". However they concede that the reported cases go beyond this. Their conclusion is that the matter is open in the House of Lords and that the opportunity might there be taken to restore to section 22(1) the full literal effect of its wording.

On our inquiring why we should not clarify the matter, we were referred to this court's decisions in *Keighley Maxted & Co* v *Bryan Durrant & Co* [1893] 1 QB 405 and *Montgomery Jones* v *Liebenthal & Co* (1898) 78 LT 406 as being the only two authorities binding upon us, although counsel rightly conceded that they might not be decisive.

Keighley Maxted & Co v *Bryan Durrant & Co.* The issue was whether there was power to remit an award for reconsideration by the arbitrators, material fresh evidence having been discovered after the award was published. Lord Esher MR, Lopes and Kay LJJ all expressed the view that section 10 of the Arbitration Act 1889 was far more limited in its scope than the literal words would suggest, but the only issue which the court had to decide was whether there was power to remit on the basis of the discovery of fresh evidence. It is no doubt powerful persuasive authority, but it binds us only to hold that the scope of the section is sufficiently wide to cover a remission on the grounds there in issue.

Montgomery Jones v *Liebenthal & Co.* Here Mr Sanderson of counsel, appearing for the respondents, put forward the argument that the jurisdiction was limited to remission on four defined grounds. The applicants' case was based upon a complaint that the arbitrators had gone wrong on a point of law. Smith LJ accepted the argument of the respondents. But Chitty LJ, having referred to *Keighley Maxted,* said:

> "It is not, however, now necessary to limit the operation of section 10 to those four grounds, for we are asked to remit the matter to the arbitrators solely upon the ground that they have gone wrong on a point of law. That, if it came within any part of the Arbitration Act, would come within section 19, [the special case section] and not section 10."

Collins LJ agreed with both judgments. This again provides powerful persuasive authority, but, in the light of the fact that Collins LJ whilst agreeing with the view of Smith LJ also agreed with Chitty LJ that it was not necessary to decide the point, I do not regard the decision as in any way tying our hands.

Against these two decisions has to be set another decision of this court in *Mutual Shipping* v *Bayshore Shipping* [1985] 1 WLR 625 ("The Montan") in which the arbitrator made, and readily admitted that he had made, an inadvertent error in awarding damages to the owners when he meant to award them to the charterers. This fell within the third of the four traditional categories of case to which section 22 undoubtedly applies, but the language of the judgments strongly suggests that every member of the court thought that the jurisdiction was far wider. Again in no way decisive, but a pointer in a different direction.

Leaving decisions of this court aside, there have been several indications by judges sitting at first instance that they thought that the jurisdiction was far wider. I refer in particular to the decision of Diplock J, then as always an acknowledged expert in the field, in *Margulies Brothers* v *Dafnis Thomaides & Co (U.K.) Ltd* (1958) 1 Lloyd's Rep 250. He said, at page 253:

> "I have no hesitation in holding that I have jurisdiction to remit an award for the payment of money so that it may be amended to put it in a form in which it will be so enforceable. If this extends the categories in which cases can be remitted to the arbitrator which were approved in *Re Montgomery Jones & Co* v *Liebenthal & Co* (1898) 78 LT 406, I will cheerfully, encouraged by Fletcher Moulton LJ in *Re Baxters* v *Midland Railway Co* (1906) 95 LT 20, so extend them."

I think that a clear distinction has to be made between the nature and scope of the remedy which Parliament has entrusted to the courts under section 22 and the use which the courts are prepared to make of it in the exercise of a judicial discretion and in the light of precedent. The limits of each might loosely be called "jurisdictional", but in truth only the former deserves that appellation.

Section 22 forms part of a series of sections designed to enable the High Court both to assist the process of settling disputes by arbitration and to supervise that process. The assistance is provided under section 4 (staying court proceedings), section 10 (power of court in certain cases to appoint an arbitrator or umpire), section 12(6) (conduct of proceedings, witnesses etc) and section 26 (enforcement of award). The supervisory role is based upon the common law and section 13 (time for making award), section 18 (costs), section 19 (taxation of arbitrators or umpires' fees), section 22 (remission), section 23 (removal of arbitrator and/or setting aside award), section 24 (relief where arbitrator is not impartial or the dispute involves question of fraud) and section 25 (power of court where arbitrator is removed or authority of arbitrator is revoked).

In ascertaining the limits of the court's jurisdiction, properly so called, I see no reason why section 22 and the other sections should not be construed as meaning what they say. Certainly so far as section 22 is concerned, there is no element of doubt or ambiguity. The jurisdiction is wholly unlimited. It may well be the case that section 8 of the Common Law Procedure Act 1854 was enacted with a view to providing a statutory alternative to "Mr Richards' clause", the terms of which I have not been able to discover, but this objective cannot limit the effect of the words used in the section in the absence of ambiguity. How that jurisdiction should be exercised is a quite different matter and to that I now turn.

Just as the courts have refused to allow the old forms of action to rule them from their graves, so I cannot accept that the exercise of judicial discretion in one century should dictate its exercise in another, although I appreciate the need over the shorter term for consistency of approach.

In *The Montan (supra)* I said at page 632:

> "Section 22 empowers the court to remit an award to an arbitrator for reconsideration. It provides the ultimate safety net whereby injustice can be prevented, but it is subject to the consideration that it cannot be used merely to enable the arbitrator to correct errors of judgment, whether on fact or law, or to have second thoughts, even if they would be better thoughts.
>
> In the instant case, the arbitrator has accidentally made a major error, which, if uncorrected, would lead to the charterers paying the owners, when it is the owners who should be paying the charterers. No court could lend the power of the state to the enforcement of such an award and no court should stand by when it has power to correct such an accidental error and I stress the word 'accidental'."

The philosophy underlying this statement of law as I saw it then, and as I still see it, is that the great distinguishing feature between litigation and arbitration is that parties voluntarily submit to the latter system of disputes resolution, save when it is imposed by statute, and as part of that choice can stipulate who shall be the judges and the procedures to be adopted. As a consequence, it is not unreasonable, although the matter can be more politely expressed, to require them to accept those judges and those procedures "warts and all". On the other hand, arbitration is not entirely a private matter, because the state stands in the background as the ultimate enforcer of the resulting award, either by means of section 26 of the Act or as a result of an action on the award. In exercising a discretion under section 22, the courts must never lose sight of this fundamental distinction or of the ultimate involvement of the state.

Another distinction which has to be borne in mind is that in litigation there is a right of interlocutory appeal at every stage, subject only to restrictions as to time and the need to obtain leave. By contrast in arbitration, subject to certain exceptions such as the power to remove an arbitrator for bias, any intervention by the court can only occur after the award has been made. This is not accidental, but stems from the fact that the parties have chosen to adopt an extracurial system for the resolution of their disputes. If the courts are not intended to intervene at the time to correct what they might perceive to be errors in the conduct of the arbitration, *a fortiori* they should not intervene retrospectively after the award has been published.

All this might suggest that, as a matter of discretion, there are no cases in which the section 22 power should be exercised. The parties having made their bed should be left to lie on it. To some extent this is true. If the arbitrator in the event is believed by one party, perhaps rightly, to have wrongly accepted the evidence of a particular witness or found for the other party on an erroneous appreciation of the weight of the evidence generally, there is no reason for the courts to intervene. Similarly if the arbitrator misinterprets the law. The aggrieved party having voluntarily invested the arbitrator with authority to ascertain the law and apply it for the facts, subject to such rights of appeal on questions of law as may be afforded by the Arbitration Act 1979, there is no reason why the courts, acting on behalf of the state, should hesitate in enforcing that award. However there are limits. Whilst it may be impossible, or at least undesirable, to seek to determine those limits, save on a case by case basis, I personally find it helpful to ask myself what in truth the parties accepted when they agreed to arbitrate, although I am far from saying that this is the exclusive touchstone.

This was the approach of Diplock J in *Margulies* v *Dafnis Thomaides & Co (UK) Ltd* (*supra*) when he held that it was an implied term of the arbitration agreement that the award would be in an enforceable form. Equally I think that it could have been said in *The Montan (supra)* that it was an implied term of the arbitration agreement that the arbitrator would not *accidentally* make an award in favour of A when he meant B, although it was certainly not an implied term that he would not intentionally, but *bona fide,* make an award in favour of A when, viewed objectively, he should have made one against B. Similarly it is probably an implied term of any arbitration agreement, unless excluded by express terms, that each party should have a fair opportunity of being heard and my own decision in *The Aristides Xilas* [1975] 2 Lloyd's Rep 402 might have been justified on this basis. However that decision and others also involve a further element of which account has to be taken, namely, the extent to which the matters complained of were induced by the action or inaction of the aggrieved party himself. In *The Aristides Xilas* in one sense the charterers were the authors of their own misfortune. They saw a sinister significance in the disappearance of Messrs Clyde & Co as their solicitors and the sudden appearance of Mr R A Clyde as the owners' replacement arbitrator and as a result did insufficient to prepare for the arbitration. On the other hand they were strangers to the London arbitration scene and did not appreciate that there was no connection between Mr Clyde and Clyde & Co. It was thus in my view just and was a proper exercise of discretion to remit the award to the arbitrators for reconsideration, although I would not have done so if the charterers had known more about London arbitration and there had accordingly been less excuse for any misunderstanding on their part.

In my judgment the remission jurisdiction extends beyond the four traditional grounds to any cases where, notwithstanding that the arbitrators have acted with complete propriety, due to mishap or misunderstanding, some aspect of the dispute which has been the subject of the reference has not been considered and adjudicated upon as fully or in a manner which the parties were entitled to expect *and* it would be inequitable to allow any award to take effect without some further consideration by the arbitrator. In so expressing myself I am not seeking to define or limit the jurisdiction or the way in which it should be exercised in particular cases, subject to the vital qualification that it is designed to remedy deviations from the route which the reference should have taken towards its destination (the award) and *not* to remedy a situation in which, despite having followed an unimpeachable route, the arbitrators have made errors of fact or law and as a result have reached a destination which was not that which the court would have reached. This essential qualification is usually underlined by saying that the jurisdiction to remit is to be invoked, if at all, in relation to procedural mishaps or misunderstandings. This is, however, too narrow a view since the traditional grounds do not necessarily involve procedural errors. The qualification is however of fundamental importance. Parties to arbitration, like parties to litigation, *are* entitled to expect that the arbitration will be conducted without mishap or misunderstanding and that, subject to the wide discretion enjoyed by the arbitrator, the procedure adopted will be fair and appropriate. What they are *not* entitled to expect of an arbitrator any more than of a judge is that he will necessarily and in all circumstances arrive at the "right" answer as a matter of fact or law. That is why there are rights of appeal in litigation and no doubt would be in arbitration were it not for the fact that in English law it is left to the parties, if they so wish, to build a system of appeal into their arbitration agreements and few wish to do so, preferring "finality" to "legality", to adopt Lord Diplock's terminology.

The arbitration

This appeal arises out of a dispute under a building contract, which was referred to arbitration under an ICE arbitration clause contained in the contract. The contractors claimed £25,000 and the building owners counterclaimed £5,000. The arbitration was protracted and accordingly costly, the arbitrators' costs alone amounting to over £10,000 to which has to be added the costs incurred by each party. Indeed the point must have been reached at which liability for costs loomed as large in the minds of the parties as success or failure on their respective claims.

This is, unfortunately, a not unfamiliar situation for which there is a classic palliative, even if it is no real remedy. It is to make a "sealed offer" of settlement to the other side — the arbitral equivalent of paying money into court — with the normal consequence that if the award is less than the amount specified in the sealed offer, the arbitrator will order the offeree to pay the offeror's costs as from the date of the offer.

This occurred in this case, the building owners making a sealed offer to pay £5,000 in settlement of all issues in the arbitration. In the event the arbitrator set off the amount which he would have awarded on the counterclaim against the amount which he would have awarded on the claim and arrived at a net sum of £4,743.51 which, by his award, he ordered the building owners to pay to the contractors. No complaint is, or can be, made at the arbitrator adopting this course.

If, when an arbitrator came to consider the amount of his substantive award, as contrasted with that relating to costs, he knew not only that an offer of settlement had been made, but also the amount of that offer, he could in some circumstances be gravely embarrassed. Hence the fact that the offer is sealed. However this does not advance matters if, in ignorance that such an offer has been made, he publishes an award which makes provision for the costs of the reference and the parties' costs on the assumption that there has been no such offer.

The standard solution to this dilemma is (a) to give the arbitrator the sealed offer, inviting him to open and consider it only after he has decided upon his substantive award or (b) to invite the arbitrator to make an interim award on the substance of the dispute and then to hold a further hearing on costs leading to a final award disposing of that aspect. Course (a) avoids the expense of a second hearing, but is only appropriate if there is no reason to believe that the arbitrator might be embarrassed in, for example, assessing damages if he knew that *some* offer had been made, even if he did not know its amount. Course (b) involves the need for, and the costs of, a further hearing, but may be justified independently of the existence of an offer of settlement if there are complex arguments on costs which may not arise if the arbitrator's decision goes one way and/or cannot sensibly be deployed unless and until it is known what view the arbitrator has taken on particular claims or parts of claims. It follows that no arbitrator should assume that an offer has been made just because he is invited to postpone a decision on costs until after he has reached a decision upon the substantive claim or claims.

How an arbitrator should take account of a sealed offer in making an award as to costs and the relevance of other factors was discussed in *Tramontana* v *Atlantic Shipping* [1978] 2 All ER 870, at pages 877-8. In the same case I suggested that any reluctance to reveal the fact that a sealed offer had been made, as distinct from the amount, would be overcome if arbitrators invited the parties to give them sealed envelopes, whose contents would reveal whether or not there had been an offer and, if so, its amount. I have no reason to dissent from what I then said, although in the context of my remarks about interest it should be noted that the law has been changed and a payment into court can now take account of liability for interest in the same way as could a sealed offer (see RSC Order 22, rule 1(8)). In this case neither the fact that a sealed offer existed nor the amount of that offer was brought to the notice of the arbitrator until after he had made his award. Nor did he appreciate that there was any reason to make an interim award. In these circumstances he proceeded at once to make a final award which very properly dealt with the costs of the reference and of the parties. Equally properly, the basic rule being that costs follow the event, he awarded that they be paid by the building owners. It is conceded that, if he had known of the offer, he would have made a different order.

The application for remission

The building owners applied to have the award remitted to the arbitrator in order that he might reconsider his award in so far as it related to costs. Hobhouse J made such an order and the contractors now appeal.

The facts

I take these from the judgment of Hobhouse J:

> "My findings of fact were and are, so far as is relevant, in the following terms: I preferred the evidence adduced by the defendants on the motion to that of the plaintiffs. I regarded the plaintiffs'

evidence as unreliable and were it not for the entry in the notebook at page 85 of the notebook of Mr Westlake, that is, the plaintiffs' solicitor, the plaintiffs would wholly fail on their allegations of fact. I accepted that nothing was said which either objectively or subjectively should have been appreciated by either the arbitrator or by the other party to the arbitration, that is, the Defendants, that the arbitrator was being asked clearly, or at all, to hold over the costs of the arbitration and to make an interim award on liability and quantum only.

As regards what was physically said, I accepted, in the light of the note, that words were at one point used by counsel that were legitimately noted as 'Hold costs over'. But that was, I found, said immediately after a matter was dealt with in relation to the costs of an amendment. It was accordingly understood to be an insignificant observation in that context by those who heard it, the arbitrator and Mr Wootton, the solicitor for the defendants.

I consider that the correct finding of fact on the balance of probabilities is that counsel, when she used those words, intended them to be used in conjunction with the argument which had just taken place in relation to the costs of the amendment but hoped that they would be sufficient to procure that all matters of costs would be held over, although she did not say that and still less did she make it clear.

As regards Mr Westlake, I consider that on the balance of probabilities he probably thought that the words were being used in relation to all the costs of the arbitration and therefore there was a misunderstanding within the plaintiffs' camp on that point. The underlying factor was that, owing to inexperience, neither of those representing the plaintiffs at the arbitration were competent or fully familiar with the correct way to handle an arbitration where costs were an important issue and there had been a sealed offer.

Counsel was very keen (and indeed she clearly had it as her highest priority) not to disclose to the arbitrator that there had been a sealed offer. She thought tactically it would damage the plaintiffs' case and therefore had to be avoided. She thought she had found a way of referring to costs in connection with the amendment point which would suffice and relieve her of the need to explain herself more fully to the arbitrator. The solicitor may have had a slightly different belief, as I have already indicated, but what happened was a failure by the plaintiffs to make their position remotely clear to the arbitrator and to the other party to the arbitration; and that arose from the way in which the plaintiffs chose to conduct the arbitration tactically in its concluding stages. Some words were used but they were used with the intent and in the context that I have found.

The outcome of the arbitration has been that the defendants have received a windfall. They lost the relevant issue but got the costs. The plaintiffs suffered a serious loss. They did so all because their counsel did not ask for an interim award or firmly grasp the nettle and say that there had been a sealed offer.

The failure to refer to the sealed offer was a tactical decision, a tactical decision not to refer to the offer at that stage. It was a deliberate tactical decision. The material was not put in. But counsel thought that she had done enough to procure a further hearing. She was mistaken in that: she had not."

The law in relation to arbitral orders as to costs

As a matter of history the jurisdiction to remit an award under section 22 has never been available to correct errors of fact or law upon the part of the arbitrator when deciding upon the terms of his award, unless these errors were apparent upon the face of the award or of a separate document forming part of the award, such as one giving the arbitrator's reasons. In this sense it is, and has always been, true to say, as Hobhouse J said in this case, that "procedure is the essence of this head of relief". However this was subject to an exception in the case of that part of an award which related to costs. Here the court was prepared to consider remission if it appeared that the arbitrator might have departed from the established rules for the exercise of a judicial discretion as to costs (see *Smeaton Hanscombe* v *Sassoon I Setty* [1953] 2 Lloyd's Rep 580, *Dineen* v *Walpole* [1969] 1 Lloyd's Rep 261 (the report speaks of "an appeal" to James J, but it must have been an application to remit or set aside in the light of the fact that the court heard evidence as to the course of the proceedings (page 267)); *Tramontana Armadora S A* v *Atlantic Shipping Co* [1978] 2 All ER 870 and *Warinco* v *Andre* [1979] 2 Lloyd's Rep 298).

As I pointed out in *Tramontana (supra)* "It is not easy to explain why an order as to costs is treated in this exceptional fashion" and, on reflection, I do not think that I did satisfactorily explain it in the passage which follows on page 873 of the report. However this may not matter as the position has undoubtedly changed following the enactment of the Arbitration Act 1979 as this court held in *Blexen Ltd* v *Percy Trentham Ltd* (*page 37 above*). There it was held that a reasoned award as to costs could only be challenged through the medium of an appeal to the High Court, leave having first been obtained under section 1 of the 1979 Act.

That would also, I think, be the only means of appeal in a case in which no reasons had been given. The fact that the order as to costs was not such as *prima facie* would have been expected to result from a judicial exercise of discretion, which used to be the foundation for the exercise of the court's powers under section 22, would now I think be regarded as a justification for ordering reasons or further reasons to be given under section 1(5) of the Act. Furthermore such an application would probably not be defeated by section 1(6), on the grounds that reasons had not been asked for prior to the making of the award, since parties cannot usually be expected to anticipate a departure from the normal principles as to costs and this might well be regarded as a "special reason" for not having asked for reasons.

All this pre-supposes, of course, that there is a *prima facie* case for alleging a departure from the normal principles. This could probably only be demonstrated by reference to what appears on the face of the award, ie a comparison between that part of the award which dealt with the substance of the dispute and that part which dealt with costs.

Nothing in this change of the law detracts from the validity of the advice given to arbitrators to volunteer their reasons, if they are departing from the normal principles applicable to costs or it is not at once apparent that they are applying them (see judgment of Devlin J in *Smeaton Hanscomb* v *Sassoon (supra)* at page 587). Giving reasons in such circumstances will avoid applications to the court by showing that the award of costs is unappealable.

This leaves out of account an arbitration agreement which is subject to an exclusion agreement. Here there is no power to order reasons or further reasons and no right of appeal in the absence of the consent of all parties (see section 3(1) of the Act). If reasons have been given, they will normally form part of the award. If they have not been given, the applicant will be driven to rely upon the operative parts of the award to demonstrate an error on the part of the arbitrator. In either event he will be seeking remission upon grounds of error of fact or law on the face of the award and this is forbidden by section 1(1) of the 1979 Act. I therefore conclude that there is now no remedy for *bona fide* error on the part of the arbitrator in the matter of costs where the arbitration is subject to an exclusion agreement and not all parties consent to an appeal.

The law generally

I have adverted to the special position in relation to arbitral orders as to costs for completeness and in order to draw attention to the change incidentally introduced by the enactment of the 1979 Act. This is not, however, a case in which it could be or is alleged that the arbitrator erred. The general law therefore applies as I have already stated it.

The case for the appellants

Mr Fernyhough accepts that, if the arbitrator had known of the sealed offer, he would have made a different order in relation to costs and that such an order would have been more favourable to the building owners. He further accepts that, to this extent, there has been a failure to achieve a just result in the arbitration. However he rightly points out, as I have already accepted, that an unjust outcome has never of itself been regarded as a justification for remission. Arbitration, like litigation, involves human judgment which is inherently fallible. The difference between the two systems of dispute resolution lies in the fact that the machinery for correcting errors is designedly much more limited in the case of arbitration than in the case of litigation. The parties have a choice whether to opt for "finality" in the form of arbitration or for "legality" in the form of litigation. Having chosen "finality", they cannot when things go wrong change their election to one in favour of "legality".

All this is quite true and would be highly relevant if in this appeal it was alleged that after a full and fair hearing the arbitrator had arrived at the "wrong" answer due to error of fact or of law. But that is not the case. However, as Mr Fernyhough also accepts, although it was challenged in the Indian Oil Appeal, the courts are entitled to intervene by ordering remission not only in the four categories of case identified in the 19th Century authorities, but also in a miscellaneous category of cases which were christened "procedural mishaps" by Mr Christopher Staughton QC (as he then was) in *G K N* v *Matbro* [1976] 2 Lloyd's Rep 555, at page 581. The main thrust of Mr Fernyhough's submissions is that what occurred on this occasion was not a "procedural mishap".

In approaching this argument it is, I think, important to remember that, apt though Staughton LJ's label of "procedural mishap" may have been, it was intended to describe a miscellany of cases in which remission had been ordered and not to delimit the extent of the jurisdiction under this head. If a case should arise in which on general principles it was right to order remission, it would be nothing to the point that this label was appropriate.

The lynchpin of Mr Fernyhough's argument is that what occurred was the result of a deliberate tactical decision by counsel then appearing for the building owners. If the same decision had been made by the building owners themselves, there would, as he submits, have been no question of remission and there was no reason why there should be a different result simply because they were represented. He goes on to paint a gloomy picture of what would occur if we should not accept his submission — parties who were disappointed with an award would at once dismiss their lawyers and seek remission alleging that the lawyers had been incompetent. The lawyers for their part would practise "defensive law".

I find it impossible to generalise. In the field of litigation errors by lawyers will sometimes be visited upon the client, eg striking out for want of prosecution or for failure to serve a writ within the time limits. On the other hand a default judgment is more likely to be set aside, if it resulted from inaction or inattention on the part of the party's lawyer rather than of the party himself. Again in the field of arbitration, account should and would be taken of the fact that a procedural mishap occurred as a result of ignorance of procedure by a disputant acting in person, which might not be so explicable or excusable in the case of one who was represented. It is a very sensitive jurisdiction which has to be exercised in the light of well-established principles, but with a careful regard to all the facts in particular cases.

If in this case counsel for the building owners had deliberately decided for tactical reasons neither to disclose the fact that a sealed offer had been made nor to ask the arbitrator to hold over any decision on costs until after he had made his award, however inexplicable such a decision might have been, there would have been little or no case for remission. But that is not this case. On a fair reading of the facts as found by the judge, counsel reached two tactical decisions. The first was to make no reference to the sealed offer. The second was to indicate in a low key way that the issue of costs should stand over. The second decision was prompted by the same consideration as the first, namely that she thought that any indication that an offer of settlement had been or *might have been* made might influence the arbitrator in his decision, adversely to her client's interests. In this I have no doubt that she did the arbitrator a grave injustice. But that is beside the point. What matters is that the tactical decision was indeed to ask that the issue of costs should stand over and counsel, mistakenly, thought that she could and would achieve this result by attaching this *sotto voce* request to a discussion on the costs of an amendment in the pleadings.

In the result the building owners have in this one respect not received a fair trial as a matter of procedure and, if it matters, I think that this can properly be described as a procedural mishap.

Mr Fernyhough's last point is that, even if this is correct, on the findings of the judge the mishap arose, if not as a result of a deliberate tactical decision, at least as a result of fault on the building owners' side and, for this reason, remission should be refused. As he frankly admits, if we were to accede to this proposition we should have to overrule the decision of Brandon J (as he then was) in *The Aros* [1978] 1 Lloyd's Rep 456 and, incidentally, my own decision in *The Aristides Xilas* [1975] 2 Lloyd's Rep 402 to which Brandon J referred. I should have not the slightest hesitation in overruling either or both decisions, if I thought that they were wrong, but I do not. I gratefully adopt the words of Brandon J at pages 463-4:

> "It was contended for the shipowner that, if and in so far as the charterers had suffered from a procedural mishap in this case, that was entirely due to their own fault, in that Professor Balestra failed to

> tell the arbitrators that he wished to put further material before them and to ask them to allow him a reasonable time for doing so. It was further contended that a party should never be entitled to have an award remitted on the ground of a procedural mishap which was entirely due to his own fault.
>
> I do not think it would be right to lay down any general rule to that effect. The court does not necessarily refuse to assist a party out of a difficulty because he has got into it by his own fault, although it may impose strict terms, with regard to costs or other matters, as a condition of giving such assistance. This is certainly the approach adopted by the court in relation to applications to set aside a default judgment, and I see no reason why it should not also be adopted, in appropriate cases, in relation to applications to remit an award: see the observations of Donaldson J in *The Aristides Xilas* [1975] 2 Lloyd's Rep 402 at page 410.
>
> I would not therefore in this case refuse the charterers' application to remit solely on the ground that the need for it is of their own making. That circumstance is, no doubt, one of the factors to be taken into account. The crucial question, however, seems to me to be whether the charterers have shown that the procedural mishap which occurred caused, or at least may well have caused, injustice to them. It is accordingly to that question, which I regard as the most important one in the case, that I now turn."

Brandon J held that there had been no injustice. In this case there is no issue as to that. A grave injustice has indeed occurred.

Hobhouse J in ordering remission imposed stringent terms as to costs, namely, that the building owners should pay the contractors' costs in or about the remission. There is no cross appeal on that aspect and, if there had been, it would have failed on the ordinary principles applicable to discretionary decisions.

I would dismiss this appeal.

RALPH GIBSON LJ: I agree that this appeal should be dismissed for the reasons given by the Master of the Rolls. In summary, therefore, I agree that, as a matter of procedure but through no fault of the arbitrator or the other party, the building owners on the facts of this case did not on the issue of costs receive a fair trial; that this resulted from what can properly be described as a procedural mishap; and that it would be inequitable to allow the award as to costs to take effect without further consideration by the arbitrator. In reaching that conclusion I took into account as a fact of significance that the failure by counsel to make clear to the arbitrator that she was in fact asking for the issue of costs to be stood over — while intending to achieve that effect by her reference to "holding costs over" in the context of the costs of an amendment — was, in the context of this case, very obviously either an unclear application to that effect or it was a blunder by counsel who must have forgotten that the sealed offer had been made. Mr Fernyhough acknowledged that there was no conceivable explanation for a failure to ask that the issue of costs be stood over other than an obvious blunder by counsel. The making of a considered decision not to secure an opportunity for consideration by the arbitrator of the sealed offer by asking for the issue of costs to be stood over can, therefore, be ruled out with a sufficient degree of certainty to justify the order of remission. I regard that as important because the jurisdiction to remit should not, in my judgment, be available to enable a party to an arbitration to repent of a considered decision by himself or his legal representatives with reference to such a matter in order for him to pursue a different course on remission to the arbitrator.

NICHOLLS LJ: I also agree that, for the reasons given by the Master of the Rolls, this appeal should be dismissed.

DU BOSKY & PARTNERS (A Firm) v SHEARWATER PROPERTY HOLDINGS plc

13 May 1991 — *Queen's Bench Division*
Official Referees' Business

His Honour Judge Esyr Lewis QC

Contract – Engagement of Quantity Surveyor – Termination – Whether contract ambiguous about instalment payments – Construction – Ambiguity

By a contract made in writing on 23 February 1989, the defendant, a developer, engaged the plaintiff firm to provide quantity surveying services in connection with the redevelopment of a canal site in Sheffield known as Cutler's Wharf. The agreement provided that the defendant should pay a total lump sum fee of £1m plus VAT, by instalments of £25,000 per month for a period of 18 months from February 1989, with the remaining instalments being agreed at the end of that period, and in accordance with the actual completion programme for the proposed development. The fee was fixed unless the construction cost varied by more than ±10% adjusted back to an October 1988 base; if this occurred, a revised fee was to be negotiated for each element affected. The engagement also incorporated the defendant's standard terms which provided by clause 18:

> "We may, in addition to any other rights and remedies which we may have, by notice, in writing to you forthwith terminate your engagement in relation to the Project.
>
> Upon any termination . . . we shall pay you any instalments of the fees and other sums due to you which have accrued due prior to the date of such termination and less any amounts previously paid by us to you."

By letter dated 13 July 1990, the defendant terminated the plaintiff's appointment as quantity surveyor to the project. At that date, the plaintiff had been paid the sum of £215,000 in accordance with the monthly payment provisions.

The plaintiff contended that it was entitled to approximately

£300,000 more than it had received since the agreement failed to provide for the plaintiff's fees if the defendant terminated the engagement before it became entitled to the full lump sum of £1m, and was ambiguous in that respect, and ought to be construed *contra proferentem* and in the light of the factual matrix of the contract. When so construed, it was contended, the provision for monthly payments was only for interim payments on account of fees earned, and was not related to the value of the services earned.

The defendant alleged that the agreement was clear and limited the plaintiff's entitlements in the event which had happened to the amount of the interim payments.

An order was made for the trial of a preliminary issue in the following terms:

> "On the basis that there was a contract between the parties incorporating the Defendant's standard terms for the engagement of consultants, and that the Defendants were entitled to terminate it on the 13th July 1989, is the effect of clause 18 of those terms such as to limit the Plaintiff's entitlement to the £215,000 already paid to them?"

***HELD**, giving judgment for the defendant:*

(1) The agreement was unambiguous. Evidence of surrounding circumstances was therefore inadmissible.

per curiam:

> "It is fundamental to the construction of contractual provisions that no evidence is admissible to explain the intention of a party to a contract when he enters into it, and that reference to surrounding circumstances or the factual matrix in which the contract is made is permissible only to establish objectively what the parties obviously intended if the language of the agreement is not unequivocally clear."

(2) The only sums payable to the plaintiff by way of fees on termination of the contract were any instalments of the fees "which have accrued due prior to the date of such termination".

(3) If there were ambiguity, then the surrounding circumstances showed that the Plaintiff's entitlement was to be paid in accordance with the instalments only.

Daniel Serota QC and Colin Manning appeared for the plaintiff, instructed by Barnett Griffin and Partners
John McDonald appeared for the defendant, instructed by McKenna and Co

Commentary

There is nothing unusual about a provision which permits the future performance of a contract to be terminated even without notice and without cause or reason being required, (see for example the RIBA Architects' Appointment (1982), clause 3.23). Where there is no such power to terminate the consequences of a purported termination are well established. If it is a repudiation the client would be liable to pay for the work done in accordance with the rights accrued under the contract and damages for other losses caused such as loss of profit: see *Edwin Hill and Partners* v *Leakcliffe Properties Ltd* (1984) 29 BLR 43 applying dicta in *Thomas* v *Hammersmith Borough Council* [1938] All ER 203 at pages 208 and 211. The present case was however not concerned with a wrongful termination but with the adequacy of the contractual remuneration. It was argued that the agreement was in some way ambiguous. Ambiguity can be latent, that is, apparent only *after* evidence has been tendered to show that what appears to be clear is in fact ambiguous, see for example the judgment of Donaldson LJ in *F G Whitley and Sons* v *Clywd County Council* (1983) 22 BLR 48 at page 57:

> "It must not be forgotten that ambiguity in the contract may be latent and, if this be alleged, evidence must not be admitted before deciding whether or not the contract is ambiguous. That may not be this case, but in general it is more satisfactory in terms of simplicity, speed and economy to admit any evidence which a party wishes to adduce, whilst reserving all questions of whether any facts so established are permissible aids to the construction of the contract."

The plaintiff's case borrowed something from the spirit of these observations. As summarised by the judge at page 81, this submission was,

> "[Mr Serota's] final and, I think, fundamental point is that the contract, not having explicitly stated that the instalment payments paid or accrued due at the date of termination of the contract were all that Mr Du Bosky was to receive, the parties must have left it open for determination, then what part of the lump sum fees Mr Du Bosky had earned at that time."

This is not a true case of latent ambiguity since this arises with instances where the contract or other document is clear — a devise to "Cousin John" seems clear enough until evidence is admitted to show that in fact there are two "Cousin Johns": see *Smith* v *Thompson* (1849) 8 CB 44. The distinction between latent and patent ambiguity is important, not only because the former permits the introduction of evidence at an earlier stage than the latter, but also because it seems that evidence of subjective intent and prior negotiations are admissible in order to construe a contract where there is latent ambiguity, see *Bank of New Zealand* v *Simpson* [1900] AC 182, but not where the ambiguity is patent, see *Prenn* v *Simmonds* [1978] 1 WLR 1381.

In this case, Judge Lewis held that the contract was clear and that therefore evidence of the matrix of fact was inadmissible and unnecessary to resolve any ambiguity.

DU BOSKY & PARTNERS (A Firm) v SHEARWATER PROPERTY HOLDINGS plc

13 May 1991

Queen's Bench Division
Official Referees' Business

His Honour Judge Esyr Lewis QC

JUDGE ESYR LEWIS QC: Mr Du Bosky is a chartered quantity surveyor who practices under the style Du Bosky & Partners who are the named plaintiffs in this action. The defendants are a public company which carries on business as property developers. I shall refer to the parties as Mr Du Bosky and Shearwater respectively.

Mr Du Bosky's claim in his reamended statement of claim is for fees and expenses earned and incurred for quantity surveying services rendered to Shearwater in connection with a development project at Cutler's Wharf, Sheffield which in fact did not come to fruition. His claim is essentially based on a quantum meruit for the value of his services up to the time when his engagement was terminated by Shearwater in July 1989.

On 18 April 1990 His Honour Judge Newey QC ordered that the hearing be restricted to issues of liability and such other issues as might be agreed between the parties in writing by 27 April 1990. The parties formulated three issues for trial pursuant to this order. I only need to set out the first issue in this judgment as I was invited by counsel to determine this issue first since its resolution, if decided in favour of Shearwater, would end the action and make unnecessary any consideration of the remaining two questions. The first issue reads as follows:

> On the basis that there was a contract between the parties incorpating the Defendants' standard terms for the engagement of consultants, and that the Defendants were entitled to terminate it on the 13th July 1989, is the effect of Clause 18 of those terms such as to limit the Plaintiffs' entitlement to the £215,000 already paid to them?

This first issue raises a point of construction. On the pleadings issues are raised as to the contract terms agreed. These issues have now been resolved by the parties and the relevant contract terms are now agreed. Before I turn to the contract terms, I consider that I should briefly state the uncontroversial background facts to the making of the agreement, which I derive from the opening by Mr Serota on behalf of the plaintiffs and the evidence of Mr Berry, who was a director of Shearwater and who was in charge of the Cutler's Wharf project when the services' contract with Mr Du Bosky was made on 23 February 1989.

In September 1986 Shearwater won a design competition promoted by the Sheffield Corporation and the British Waterways Board for the re-development of a canal-side site known as Cutler's Wharf. Shearwater had obviously worked on the preparation of a scheme for some time before this and during this time Mr Pearce, who was Shearwater's managing director, invited Mr Du Bosky to take part in the preparation of the scheme in his capacity as a quantity surveyor. It was recognised by Mr Du Bosky that his initial involvement was purely speculative in the sense that he was aware that he would receive no fees for any early quantity surveying services which he provided. However, there came a time when Mr Du Bosky considered that he was entitled to a firm agreement as to the payment of fees and the contract made in February 1989 was the eventual outcome. At this time the development scheme was still speculative from the point of view of Shearwater and no building contract had been made or indeed ever was made. In June, 1990 Shearwater abandoned the project. In February, 1989 it was envisaged that the development would be carried out in stages, the first stage being designated Phase 1A. By February, 1989 Mr Du Bosky had done a substantial amount of work on the project, mainly in connection with Phase 1A.

The negotiations leading up to the agreement made on 23 February 1989 began with a letter dated 24 January 1989 from Mr Du Bosky to Mr Berry in which he proposed, inter alia, that:

> "The total fee to be paid for the Quantity Surveying Services based on the work schedule on Budget 9 will be £1,000,000.00 excluding VAT. This sum does not include for work carried out under the heading of 'Contingencies' and a further £50,000.00 fee is requested in respect of these works."
> On 27 January 1989 Mr Berry replied saying, inter alia, that: "I would therefore expect that the £1,000,000.00 proposed would be the most that would be payable on the basis of the presently proposed development including the 4% or 5% contingency allowance".

I need only to refer briefly to the contents of one more letter to which I was referred by Mr Serota. On 13 February 1989 Mr Du

Bosky wrote to Mr Berry. I quote one paragraph from this letter:

> "Happily your tender was successful, and over the last three years the scheme has progressed to a stage where building will commence. Throughout this time, my practice has produced detailed estimates and cost plans, countless financial appraisals of various alternatives, and attended goodness knows how many meetings. All this work has been carried out accurately and speedily, and in no way have we been found wanting."

It is clear from this correspondence that Mr Du Bosky was seeking a lump sum fee for services covering the period of the whole of the proposed development and he had prepared a number of estimates of the cost of works.

By a letter dated 13 July 1990 Shearwater terminated Mr Du Bosky's appointment as quantity surveyor to the project. It is accepted that Shearwater were entitled to determine his appointment under the contract without giving any reasons. Mr Du Bosky has been paid £215,000 by Shearwater for his services. Shearwater say that the contract does not entitle Mr Du Bosky to any more money but Mr Du Bosky's claim is that he is entitled to over £300,000 more than he has received.

Mr Serota called no witnesses on behalf of Mr Du Bosky in relation to the present issue, but put in evidence a number of documents from an agreed bundle. On behalf of Shearwater Mr McDonald called Mr Berry as a witness. His signed witness statement was put in as his evidence in chief pursuant to an order made by Judge Newey. His witness statement which he verified, was very briefly supplemented in chief by oral evidence and he was cross examined by Mr Serota. Mr Serota submitted that, as the first issue was one of construction only of a contract, the terms of which were agreed, no oral evidence was necessary, although he did not object to Mr Berry being called. He reserved the right to object to parts of the evidence contained in Mr Berry's witness statement. In the result he did not formulate any specific objection to the evidence of Mr Berry following my indication that, in my judgment, some of the evidence contained in Mr Berry's witness statement was plainly inadmissible in the context of the first issue since it was directed to Shearwater's intention in making the contract for payment of fees to Mr Du Bosky. In my judgment, it was permissible to call Mr Berry as a witness to give evidence of the background leading to the making of the contract in February 1989. I do not consider that it is necessary for me to analyse the contents of his witness statement. Substantial parts of it are, in my view, plainly inadmissible on the construction point that I have to decide, but I consider that his evidence was admissible in so far as it sets the scene in which the contract of February 1989 was made.

The Contract

The contract terms were agreed orally at a meeting between Mr Pearce and Mr Berry on behalf of the defendants and Mr Du Bosky on 23 February 1989. These terms are now agreed between the parties and are as set out in a document prepared by Mr McDonald. They are as follows:

1. By the agreement:

(1) The defendants engaged the plaintiffs to act as their quantity surveyors for a development proposed by them (the defendants) and/or Cutlers Wharf Limited at Cutler's Wharf, Sheffield.

(2) The defendants agreed to pay the plaintiffs a total lump sum fee of £1,000,000 plus VAT to be paid by instalments of £25,000 per month to be paid for a period of eighteen months from February 1989, with the remainder of the instalments being agreed at the end of that period and in accordance with the actual completion programme for the proposed development.

(3) Fee sums were fixed unless construction cost for any element of the proposed development (as set out in a document prepared by a Mr Berry on behalf of the defendants) varied by more than + or – 10%, when adjusted back to October 1988 base. When this occurred, a revised fee was to be negotiated for each particular element affected.

(4) The said engagement was on the defendants' standard terms for the engagement of consultants, in the version marked "Draft/swb/ab/10.88" sent by the defendants to the plaintiffs by letter dated 8 August 1988.

It is also common ground that it was agreed at the meeting on 23 February 1989 that the sum of £90,000 which had already been paid to Mr Du Bosky should be credited against the lump sum fee of £1,000,000. Finally, it is also common ground that by an exchange of letters between Mr Berry and Mr Du Bosky, each dated 8 March 1989, it was agreed that the instalments of £25,000 would be due and payable on the last day of each month from February 1989 and that an invoice enclosed by Mr Du Bosky in a letter dated 2 March 1989 for the sum of £50,000 plus VAT would be met and would represent "the fee due for February and March of 1989 at the rate of £25,000 per month". Mr Berry's letter also confirmed the provision set out in paragraph (2) *above* that the instalments of £25,000 would be paid for a period of eighteen months from February 1989 with the remainder of the instalments being agreed as stated in paragraph (2).

Shearwater's Standard Terms

The issue formulated for resolution refers only to clause 18 of Shearwater's standard terms for the engagement of consultants, which are agreed as governing Mr Du Bosky's engagement. However, other clauses have been referred to in the course of argument and I shall refer to them. I also consider it is necessary that I should briefly describe the general effect of the standard terms so that clause 18 may be put in context.

Clause 1 provides that "You shall provide professional services as defined in Appendix 2 as and when from time to time may be necessary ..." Appendix 2 is divided into three parts. The first is headed "Pre-Construction Services" and the second "Construction Services". These two parts set out in some detail what are in substance the usual range of services which a quantity surveyor would perform in the periods before and after a building contract is concluded. The third part deals with particular services "to be performed by the quantity surveyor under and in accordance with his agreement from time to time as may be necessary or as may be required by the client ..."

There is no need for me to deal with any of the detail contained in Appendix 2. It is plain that it deals with the whole scope of the services which the quantity surveyor would be expected to perform from the time of his engagement before the making of a building contract to the end of the project for which he was engaged, including the agreement of the builder's final account.

Clause 7 provided in its first sentence that "We agree to pay you for your services the lump sum fee stated in Appendix 1". Appendix 1 was not filled in and, as appears above, the lump sum fee was independently agreed at the meeting on 23 February 1989.

Clause 8 provides as follows:

> "It is agreed that we will pay the fee referred to in paragraph 7 above by instalments as specified in Appendix 1. Provided that we shall be entitled to amend the schedule of instalment payments stipulated in Appendix 1 in consultation with you if for any reason performance of your services is delayed, disrupted or suspended."

The instalments payable were not specified in Appendix 1 but were again agreed at the meeting on 23 February 1989.

Clause 11 reads in so far as it is relevant:

> "The lump sum fee shall, except as provided below and in paragraph

> 12, be deemed to be inclusive payment for all of your services in connection with the Project and for all costs and expenses which you incur in relation to them:
>
> (i) disbursements may be reimbursable to you where so stated in Appendix 1." [In fact Appendix 1 was not completed in this respect.]
>
> "(ii) if the nature and scope of the project is varied at any time as a result of our instructions, we may, at our discretion, amend the lump sum fee to reflect the increase or decrease in work resulting from such variation."

The two paragraphs of clause 18 which are relevant to the construction issue and central to it read as follows:

> "We may, in addition to any other rights and remedies which we may have, by notice in writing to you forthwith terminate your engagement in relation to the Project.
>
> Upon any termination and subject to any set-offs or deductions which we may be entitled to make by virtue of any breach by you of your obligations, we shall pay you any instalments of the fees and other sums due to you which have accrued due prior to the date of such termination and less any amounts previously paid by us to you."

The Submissions

In summary, Mr Serota's submissions on behalf of Mr Du Bosky were these. His primary submission is that clause 18 does not say what is to be done about Mr Du Bosky's fees if Shearwater terminated his engagement before he became entitled to the full lump sum of £1,000,000 and is ambiguous in its terms in this respect. He argues that this is an ambiguity emphasised by other provisions contained in the standard terms and that clause 18 should therefore be construed *contra proferentem* and in the light of the factual matrix or setting of the contract. In short, he contends that clause 18 cannot be construed as meaning that Mr Du Bosky was to receive no more than the instalments of fees which had been paid at the time when his engagement was terminated. He submits that the relevant factual matrix in this case is that Mr Du Bosky was engaged to provide services for a development which would inevitably extend over a substantial period of time and that the instalments of fees were a mere mechanism providing a regular cash flow to Mr Du Bosky and a regular known commitment to Shearwater unrelated to the actual value of the services provided by Mr Du Bosky in any month when an instalment was paid. In support of his submission that clause 18 is ambiguous Mr Serota has made a number of points. First, he submits that, had it been intended that Mr Du Bosky's right to payment on termination of the contract was to be restricted to the instalment payments already made, it would have been unnecessary to refer in clause 18 to "other sums due to you which have accrued due prior to the date of such termination", since on Shearwater's approach all that needed to be ascertained on termination was what monthly instalments of £25,000 had accrued before termination became effective. Secondly, he submits that the contract provided that the lump sum payment was to be adjusted if the construction cost for any element of the proposed development varied by more than 10% either upwards or downwards. This submission is based on a document produced and laid on the table, in the words of Mr Berry, when the contract was made on 23 February 1989. The negotiation of Mr Du Bosky's fees on 23 February 1989 was, I find, undoubtedly made on the basis of the estimated cost of the whole of the Cutler's Wharf development, which had been made by Mr Du Bosky. Had the project proceeded to fruition, therefore, the lump sum payment might have had to be revised by reference to that document, which set out the estimated costs at that time of the whole proposed project. The essence of Mr Serota's submission on this point is that it could not have been intended that, if termination of the engagement of Mr Du Bosky occurred at a time when a lump sum required reconsideration by Shearwater because the scope and cost of an element in the proposed works had changed, his fees should be restricted to the instalments of his fees which had accrued due. He argues that the instalment payments are to be regarded simply as interim payments on account of fees earned and are not related to the value of the services rendered. His final and, I think, fundamental point is that, the contract not having explicitly stated that the instalment payments paid or accrued due at the date of termination of the contract were all that Mr Du Bosky was to receive, the parties must have left it open for determination then what part of the lump sums fees Mr Du Bosky had earned at that time.

For Shearwater, the substance of the argument advanced by Mr McDonald was this. The court should construe clause 18 by reference solely to the words used in the clause. The natural meaning of the words used in clause 18, argues Mr McDonald, are that, on termination of the agreement by Shearwater, Mr Du Bosky is only entitled to payment of the agreed monthly instalments of fees which have accrued due together with "other sums due to you which have accrued due prior to the date of termination". He submits that these "other sums" must be different from fees and that, accordingly, as Mr Du Bosky's claim is for fees additional to the amounts paid by instalments which had accrued due before termination, he is not entitled to any further sum by way of fees. It is of course common ground that all the monthly instalments which had accrued when the contract was terminated on 13 July 1989 had been paid. He submits that "other sums" is not otiose since it could refer to Appendix 1 of Shearwater's standard terms which refer in paragraph 6 to disbursements, although this paragraph was not completed, and to sums identified in clause 11 of the standard terms, particularly clause 11(ii) set out *above* and clause 11(iii) which states that "if you are required to perform extra work as a result of any damage to or destruction of the Project whilst under construction, we shall pay you a fair and reasonable amount in respect of such extra work". He contends that this interpretation of clause 18 of the standard terms produces a reasonable result and that, if the case advanced on behalf of Mr Du Bosky is correct, then a complicated investigation is required to determine what a proper valuation of Mr Du Bosky's services to the date of termination of his engagement is. It was implicit in his submission that there was no ambiguity in the express terms of the contract made on 23 February 1989 but that, if reference was necessary to the surrounding circumstances, the intention was that Mr Du Bosky would only earn the full lump sum fee if the whole envisaged Cutler's Wharf project was carried out to completion and that the instalment payments of £25,000 monthly would fairly compensate him for his services if they were terminated before the lump sum fee was earned, given the fact that the contract governing Mr Du Bosky's fees entitled Shearwater to terminate the contract for his services at any time and that when this contract was made there was no commitment by Shearwater to Mr Du Bosky that the development project would be carried out so that he would earn his lump sum fee. No building contract had been concluded by the time of the agreement between Shearwater and Mr Du Bosky on 23 February 1989 and the project was then plainly still in the potential or speculative stage.

Conclusions

It is fundamental to the construction of contractual provisions that no evidence is admissible to explain the intention of a party to a contract when he entered into it and that reference to surrounding circumstances or the factual matrix in which the contract is made is permissible only to establish objectively what the parties obviously intended if the language of the agreement is not unequivocally clear. This seems to me to be the effect of the passages from *Chitty on Contracts*, 26th Edn, to which I was referred by Mr McDonald. In *Prenn* v *Simmonds* [1971] 1 WLR 1381 Lord Wilberforce said this at page 1383:

"The time has long passed when agreements, even those under seal,

> were isolated from the matrix of facts in which they were set and interpreted on internal linguistic considerations."

I have also been referred to a passage in Lord Reid's speech in *L G Schuler A G* v *Wickman Machine Tools Sales Ltd* [1974] AC 235 where he said at page 251:

> "But we must remember that we are seeking to discover intention as disclosed by the contract as a whole ... The fact that a particular construction leads to a very unreasonable result must be a relevant consideration. The more unreasonable the result the more unlikely it is that the parties can have intended it, and if they did intend it the more necessary it is that they shall make the intention abundantly clear."

I have come to the conclusion that clause 18, in the light of the other terms of the standard agreement to which I have been referred, is not ambiguous. In my judgment, it provides that the only sums payable to Mr Du Bosky by way of fees on termination of the contract are any instalments of the fees "which have accrued due prior to the date of such termination". I accept Mr McDonald's argument that "other sums" relates to sums other than fees which were to be paid by instalments under clause 18. It has to be remembered that the agreement was to govern the relations of the parties to the end of the project. Had the project proceeded to its end, Mr Du Bosky might have become entitled to fees for extra work in the circumstances envisaged in clause 11(iii). In my view, clause 18 does clearly limit the entitlement to fees to the amount of the instalments which have accrued due at the time of termination. I also consider, again in the light of the fact that the agreement was to govern the payments to be made to Mr Du Bosky to the end of the project, that the provision that the sums payable were to be "less any amounts previously paid by us to you" is apt to embrace payments which were made to Mr Du Bosky before the date of the agreement of 23 February 1989 and which might have been made after the end of the initial instalment agreement, which was only to be effective from eighteen months from February 1989.

It seems to me to be important to the construction of clause 18 that the agreement of 23 February 1989 was for the payment of a lump sum for all services described in Appendix 2 of the standard terms to the very end of the project if it had been proceeded with and if Mr Du Bosky's services were retained to the end. It was never agreed that he would be entitled to a fee for any particular element of the whole project, although it appears that the lump sum fee was negotiated on 23 February 1989 by reference to the then estimated costs of the whole project. As I have already indicated, the document laid on the table in the discussion which took place then is only of contractual force in so far as it set out the estimated cost of each element of the project at that time for the purpose of determining whether a variation of the lump sum fee was to be made if the cost of any element eventually proved to be over 10% more or less than its then estimated cost. I find it difficult to see how it can be found that the parties intended that Mr Du Bosky should receive a fair value for the services he had performed if his engagement was ended before he became entitled to the lump sum when there was no provision in the agreement as to the basis for valuation of his services in those circumstances, when it could have easily been made. I agree with Mr McDonald's submission that the provision in the contract for payments to be made by monthly instalments for a period of eighteen months from February 1989 and for the instalment arrangement to be re-negotiated then was not simply a mechanism for making interim payments with a view to revaluation of the works but was definitive of Mr Du Bosky's entitlement to payment of fees if his engagement was ended by Shearwater under the provisions of clause 18.

If there is any ambiguity in clause 18 with regard to the valuation and payment of fees to Mr Du Bosky, contrary to the view I have formed, I consider that the surrounding circumstances in which the contract of 23 February 1989 was made reinforce my conclusion. First, it is clear that Mr Du Bosky did and expected to do a substantial amount of quantity surveying work before the agreement as to payment was made without expecting payment for it. What he hoped for was an engagement under which he would earn fees if the speculative project was carried through. Secondly, when the contract for his services was made on 23 February 1989, the project had not reached the stage where any building contract had been made and the possibility, which became the fact, was that the Cutler's Wharf project would be aborted by Shearwater so that Mr Du Bosky would not be able to earn the lump sum fee based on the estimated cost of the whole project. Thirdly, it is plain that the lump sum fee was only to be earned and paid in instalments over the whole period which would be required to complete the project. I accept Mr Berry's evidence, as relevant to the surrounding circumstances, that in February 1989 Phase 1A of the works were expected to start in May 1989 and to take eighteen months to complete and that completion of the whole development project would have taken about three and a half years from February 1989. In this context, I do not consider that the provision that Mr Du Bosky should be paid by instalments at the rate of £25,000 a month without any valuation of his services in any given period to be unreasonable. The central fact is that he was never going to receive the lump sum fee unless the whole project was undertaken to a conclusion and his services used to the end. In my view, the instalment provisions made in the agreement of 23 February 1989 in clause 18, the definitive and final remuneration provisions of the contract in the event of its determination.

For these reasons, therefore, I consider that the answer to the first issue for determination is that the effect of clause 18 is to limit Mr Du Bosky's entitlement to the sum of £215,000 already paid to him.

IAN ROSCOE WATTS and LESLIE MARY SAMUEL WATTS v RALPH MORROW

30 July 1991 *Court of Appeal*

The President, Ralph Gibson, and Bingham LJJ

Negligent pre-purchase survey – Nature and measure of damages recoverable.

In August 1986 the plaintiffs engaged the defendant to provide a full structural survey of Nutford Farm House, Blandford, Dorset which they intended to buy. In a long and detailed report the defendant stated that the property was "stable and in a good condition", and that the defects could be remedied in the course of "regular maintenance required of a building of its age and type". In response to subsequent enquiries by the plaintiffs the defendant said that the price was fair and that none of the necessary repairs would involve substantial expenditure. The house was bought by the plaintiffs in April 1987 for £177,500. Later major defects were found in it requiring *inter alia* the construction of a new roof, and the replacement of windows.

In November 1987 a writ was issued against the defendant alleging negligence in failing to identify and inform the plaintiffs of the defective condition of the house. The plaintiffs claimed the difference between the price paid and the value of the property, the cost of repairs, expenditure on alternative accommodation and the removal and storage of furniture, and losses resulting from the investigation of the defects. Damages were claimed, in addition, for "distress, worry, vexation and inconvenience."

Judge Bowsher QC, sitting as an official referee, accepted the plaintiffs' evidence, and as to the measure of damage for the consequences of the negligent survey, held, that in the circumstances of the case damages should be assessed on the basis of the cost of repair rather than diminution of value (which was £15,000). He awarded damages of £33,961 for the cost of repair, and £4,000 for each plaintiff representing the distress and inconvenience suffered by each of them. He awarded interest at the Judgment Act rate of 15%.

The defendant appealed only as to the assessment of damages on the grounds: (1) that the judge was wrong in law to have awarded damages on the basis of cost of repairs rather than diminution in value; (2) it was wrong in law to award the damages for distress and inconvenience alternatively, the award was excessive; (3) the interest rate was excessive.

***HELD**: allowing the appeal in part,*

(1) The principle that a plaintiff is entitled to a sum which will place him in as good a position as if the contract for the survey had been properly discharged, underlay the decision of the Court of Appeal in *Phillips* v *Ward* [1956] 1 WLR 471; 4 BLR 142. The recoverable loss was limited to diminution in value i.e. the difference between the price paid (or the value of the property in an assumed good condition) and its actual value in the light of defects which should have been reported to the plaintiff (in this case £15,000.) Accordingly the award of £33,961 would be set aside and an amount of £15,000 substituted. *Phillips* v *Ward* [1956] 1 WLR 471; 4 BLR 142; *Perry* v *Sidney Phillips* [1982] 1 WLR 1297; 22 BLR 120 *applied*: *Hipkins* v *Cotton* [1989] 2 EGLR 157; *Syrett* v *Carr & Neave,* (noted at page 121 *infra*) *overruled.*

(2) A contract to carry out a prepurchase survey was not a contract to provide peace of mind or freedom from distress. General damages for mental distress were not recoverable unless caused by physical discomfort or inconvenience resulting from breach of contract. Applying that principle the proper award was excessive and since the plaintiffs' only discomfort occurred during eight weekends the award should be reduced to £750 for each plaintiff.

(3) The judge had been entitled to make an award of interest at the rate of 15% in the exercise of his discretion and such an award was not an award which no reasonable judge could make.

Rupert Jackson QC and Iain Hughes appeared for the appellant, instructed by Pinsent & Co
Phillip Naughton QC and Jonathan Acton Davis appeared for the respondents, instructed by Goodman Derrick & Co

Commentary
This is an important case not simply in relation to the question of damages for negligent prepurchase surveys but also in relation to damages for inconvenience.

In his judgment Judge Bowsher QC had distinguished the decision of the Court of Appeal in *Phillips* v *Ward* [1956] 1 WLR 471; 4 BLR 142 and *Perry* v *Sidney Phillips & Co* [1982] 1 WLR 1297; 22 BLR 120 on the basis that in those cases the defects had been discovered shortly after the purchase and that therefore the plaintiffs had had a real choice between selling the property again at its true value (and making a loss which was less than the cost of repairs) or doing the repairs. He had adopted the same reasoning in his earlier decision in the case of *Syrett* v *Carr & Neave*, the judgment in which is for convenience included in this volume as a Note (at page 121 below). In that case Judge Bowsher said (see page 131 below)

> "That is not the case here where instant resale of the property would not have left the purchaser with a loss less than the cost of repairs and more importantly, the purchaser had no reason to make an instant sale of the property because she did not know of the defect until two years after moving in and by then she was so heavily involved with the property that it was reasonable for her to keep it and repair it. It seems to me to be wholly artificial to tell a plaintiff that her damage is to be measured in relation to a loss which she would have taken by making a sale two years before she learned that there was a loss to be realised. That does not seem to me to be what the Court of Appeal was saying in *Phillips* v *Ward* on the facts of that case."

However the difference in value approach was adopted by the Court of Appeal in *Phillips* v *Ward* because this reflected the obligation undertaken by the valuer and the consequence of reliance upon the fulfilment of that obligation by the purchaser i.e. the purchase of the property at a higher price than would have been paid had its true condition been known. It was part of the *ratio* of the decision in *Phillips* v *Ward* that damage was to be assessed at the date of purchase so what the purchaser might do on discovering the defects is irrelevant. The point was expressly dealt with by Oliver LJ in *Perry* v *Sidney Phillips* (1982) 22 BLR 120 at page 129, by Kerr LJ at page 131 and by Lord Denning MR at page 125.

Nevertheless since *Phillips* v *Ward* remains unpalatable to claimants the Court of Appeal looked again at the point of issue. Most claimants find it difficult to believe that they are adequately compensated by the award of the diminution in value, plus interest — unless it is equivalent to the cost of reinstatement which in many instances is the case. The house will usually be subject to a large mortgage and the plaintiffs will have to find the cost of repair out of their own pocket. If the market has not risen it seems unrealistic to expect the houseowner to have a real choice between repair and resale. The cost of putting right the defects will appear to result in a loss greater than the loss in capital value. Thus the plaintiffs in this action saw that their house which cost them £177,500 to buy (they paid £2,500 more than the offered price to secure it) appeared to have a net value to them of about £143,500 (deducting £34,000 for the cost of repairs). Yet on *Phillips* v *Ward* case and *Perry* v *Phillips* case they would only receive £15,000 towards their perceived loss. However as Bingham LJ stated in his judgment (at page 119) if they were to receive £34,000 they would not be placed in the same position as if the surveyor had done his job properly but in a much better one since they would effectively have got a house worth £162,500 for £143,500. For this reason even if *Phillips* v *Ward* did not bind the Court of Appeal it would have been surprising if the same conclusion had not been reached. Judge Bowsher's conclusion therefore required the defendant to pay a sum greater than the amount of money which would put the plaintiffs in the same position as they would have been in had the contract been properly performed.

It may however still be argued that in reality the plaintiffs had a choice. Either they could decide to cut their losses and sell the house for £162,500, spend the money on property value elsewhere and recover their £15,000 diminution value from Mr Morrow (£162,500 + £15,000 = £177,500), or alternatively they could decide to stay in the house and spend the money necessary to obtain a property value of £177,500 at this house. The cost of doing that is the cost of repairs £34,000. Whichever of the two alternatives Mr and Mrs Watts' adopted they end up with property value of £177,500 which would be precisely the property value they would have obtained one way or another had the report been properly prepared. The real issue therefore is whether or not it was reasonable for Mr and Mrs Watts to spend the considerably greater sum of £34,000 on the cost of repair rather than incur the costs of selling the house they had bought and re-purchasing elsewhere (with all the attendant costs of estate agents, stamp duty, solicitors, Land Registry fees, removal costs etc.) In some cases the cost of repairs will be so disproportionate to the costs incurred in taking the alternative course of selling the property and obtaining property value elsewhere that the plaintiff who took the former course would be held not to have mitigated his damage. However in many cases the inconvenience to the plaintiff from re-sale would outweigh a marginal increase in cost involved in staying in the house and carrying out works of repair. It is after all the defendant, the contract breaker, who has placed the plaintiff in the position where such difficult choices have to be taken. Why should it be assumed that the Plaintiff can act as if he were a property developer? On this view the reasoning of the Court of Appeal ought to be regarded as wrong, but only on the basis that it does not raise an issue of principle but underlyingly an issue of fact.

Similar issues were considered by the Court of Appeal in *Hayes* v

Dodd [1990] 2 All ER 816. In that case the purchasers' solicitors assured them that they had a right of way to the land which they were intending to purchase for the purpose of using it for their business. In fact two days after completion of the purchase it was discovered that there was no right of way. It was impossible to transact the plaintiffs' business from the land and it was clear that had the true position been known the plaintiffs would not have proceeded. However, they had proceeded. Staughton LJ said as follows at page 818.

> "The first question in this appeal relates to the basis on which damages should be assessed. Like Hirst J I start with the principle stated by Lord Blackburn in *Livingstone* v *Rawyards Coal Co* (1880) 5 App Cas 25 at 39:
>
> > '. . . you should as nearly as possible get at that sum of money which will put the party who has been injured, or who has suffered, in the same position as he would have been in if he had not sustained the wrong for which he is now getting his compensation or reparation.'
>
> One must therefore ascertain the actual situation of the plaintiffs and compare it with their situation if the breach of contract had not occurred.
>
> What then was the breach of contract? It was not the breach of any warranty that there was a right of way: the defendant solicitors gave no such warranty. This is an important point: see *Perry* v *Sidney Phillips & Son (a firm)*, [1982] 1 WLR 1297. The breach was of the solicitors' promise to use reasonable skill and care in advising their clients. If they had done that, they would have told the plaintiffs that there was no right of way; and it is clear that, on the receipt of such advice, the plaintiffs would have decided not to enter into the transaction at all. They would have bought no property, spent no money and borrowed none from the bank.
>
> That at first sight is the situation which one should compare with the actual financial state of the plaintiffs. I will call this the 'no-transaction method'. There are, however, authorities which show that instead one takes for the first element in the comparison the situation which the plaintiff would have been in if the transaction had gone through in accordance with his legitimate expectations. This I call the 'successful-transaction method'. Thus, in *Perry*'s case, the plaintiff recovered from negligent surveyors the difference between the value of the house at the date when he bought it if it had not been defective and its actual value at that date. However, it appears to have been found, or assumed, in that case that the plaintiff would still have bought the house if he had been given correct advice as to its condition, albeit at a lower price. It was not a case where he would never have entered into the transaction at all.
>
> . . .
>
> The difference between the two methods is unlikely to be of importance in a case which concerns some commodity that is readily

> saleable, such as peas or beans, and if there is no difficulty or delay in ascertaining that a breach has occurred.
>
> . . .
>
> However, this case is not concerned with a readily saleable commodity: it took the plaintiffs nearly five years from the date of their purchase to dispose of the maisonette, and another year expired before they were free from the obligations imposed by the lease of the workshop and yard. During all that period they were incurring expenses, such as rent and other items, together with interest on the money which they had borrowed from the bank. Furthermore, they did not receive, until the first year had almost expired, any acknowledgement by the defendants that there was in fact no right of way; that only happened on 6 July 1983, whereas they had completed their purchase on 28 July 1982 and the right of way had first been challenged two days later.
>
> I am quite satisfied that Hirst J was entitled to award damages in this case on the no-transaction basis, and that he was right to do so. Indeed it may well be that the plaintiffs were, as he held, entitled to elect between that method and the successful-transaction method; but I need not express any concluded view on that. So they should recover all the money which they spent, less anything which they subsequently recovered, provided always that they acted reasonably in mitigating their loss. But they were quite properly denied any sum for the profit which they would have made if they had operated their business successfully."

Whilst there is no absolute principle prohibiting the use of the "no transaction approach" (see the judgment of Bingham LJ in *County Personnel Limited* v *Pulver* [1987] 1 WLR 916) it will not normally apply: it might do so if, whatever the notional diminished value, the property was not readily saleable.

The application of the *Phillips* v *Ward* principle has caused some judicial regrets. For example, even in cases in which the measure of damage has been the diminution in value there have been awards of the costs of alternative accommodation whilst non emergency works are carried out, see for example *Treml* v *Ernest W Gibson & Partners* (1984) 272 EG 68. If this is not double counting it is explicable on the basis that, but for the negligent survey, remedial works would have been carried out before the plaintiff moved in. In *Bigg* v *Howard Son & Gooch* (1990) 12 EG 111 Judge Hicks QC disallowed such a claim where it had been taken into account in the diminution of value figure.

The second point in this case may perhaps prove to be of equal practical importance as its application extends beyond contracts for prepurchase surveys. People are understandably upset if they have to live in a defective house. To what extent can general damages for the loss and inconvenience suffered by them be recovered? As is apparent from the judgments, the key issue depends upon the object of the contract. Was it one by which the contract breaker either expressly or impliedly undertook to provide "peace of mind or freedom from distress?" If it was, then general damages will be recoverable since they will be the loss which arises naturally in the usual course of things from failure to comply with the obligations under the contract. Thus into this category there clearly fall contracts for holidays: *Jarvis* v *Swans Tours* [1973] 1 QB 233; *Jackson* v *Horizon Holidays* [1975] 1 WLR 1468. (However such damages will not extend simply to compensation for the aggravation caused by the very existence of the dispute which leads to the litigation.) Some contracts in connection with the purchase or construction of a house or other building may fall into this category, but if the contract does not do so then, as the Court of Appeal held, damages are recoverable for physical inconvenience and discomfort or other mental distress, only if they are caused by physical discomfort or inconvenience resulting from breach of contract, and not otherwise. Furthermore the amount of such damages should be modest: the Court of Appeal applied what Lord Denning MR said in *Perry* v *Phillips* [1982] 1 WLR 1297 at pages 302-303; see also 22 BLR 120 at page 127. As a result on the facts of this case the plaintiffs' compensation was limited to £750 each for the week-ends in which they lived in the house whilst the repair work was being carried out all around them. The Court of Appeal held that the award was excessive by any standards. A useful summary of recent cases in which awards have been made for inconvenience is set out at page 116 of the judgment.

Finally, the Court of Appeal declined to interfere with the exercise of the judge's discretion to award interest at 15%, albeit that it had apparently been fixed at the rate set out in the Judgment Acts and not at the rate of the short-term investment account. The selection of an interest rate is a matter of discretion and, unless exercised on a wrong principle, will not be disturbed by the Court of Appeal.

IAN ROSCOE WATTS and LESLIE MARY SAMUEL WATTS v RALPH MORROW

30 July 1991 *Court of Appeal*

The President, Ralph Gibson, and Bingham LJJ

RALPH GIBSON LJ: This is an appeal by the defendant, Mr Ralph Morrow FRICS, a building surveyor, against the judgment obtained by the plaintiffs, Mr & Mrs Watts, on 9 November 1990, after trial of the action by His Honour Judge Bowsher QC. The action arose out of a negligent survey report by the defendant made in August 1986 upon Nutford Farm House, Blandford in Dorset which the plaintiffs were proposing to buy and thereafter bought. The judgment awarded £33,961.35 for the cost of certain repairs to the house, with £12,839.87 for interest; and £8,000 (£4,000 for each plaintiff) for "distress and inconvenience" with interest of £477.81. At the trial liability was in issue but the defendant's appeal is on damages only. He contends, firstly, that the judge was wrong in law to award damages based upon the cost of repairs and that the award should have been, on the basis of diminution in value or excess purchase price paid, in the sum of £15,000; secondly, that any award for distress and inconvenience was wrong in law, alternatively that the award of £8,000 was excessive; and, thirdly, that the award of interest was based upon an excessive rate.

The case raises questions of general importance both for surveyors of houses and for those who buy houses in reliance upon survey reports. The defendants contend that the learned judge has disregarded the rule which, since 1956 at least, has been generally held to apply to such cases as this. The plaintiffs assert that there is no such rule or, if there is, that it is wrong to apply it in this case. It is necessary to set out the facts in some detail.

Summary of the facts

(i) Mr Watts is a stockbroker employed by Barclays de Zoete Wedd UK Equities Ltd. Mrs Watts, a solicitor, is a director of Kleinwort

Benson Ltd, merchant bankers. In 1986 they were married and living in a house in Cloudesley Road, Islington. They decided to look for a country house for use at weekends and holidays.

(ii) Their case at trial was that they both wanted a house which would be, so far as possible, trouble-free and into which they could move without the need for any substantial works of repair. It was to be a second home for use at weekends and holidays. Each had a substantial income but considered that, although they could buy a new house within a budget of £170,000, they could not afford to buy a house which required the carrying out of any expensive repairs. Further, they did not have the time or energy to get involved in doing up a house which required extensive repairs or improvements.

(iii) Mr Watts found and "fell in love with" the house. It was a larger house than Mrs Watts had expected to buy but, as she said, "it was very beautiful, a house with a heart and difficult to resist", built in the 18th and 19th century. The house is substantial with three quarters of an acre of garden and three acres of paddock. It is near the river Stour and the vendor was willing to let the purchaser have some fishing rights.

(iv) The asking price of the house was £175,000. There was another prospective purchaser. The plaintiffs decided to offer £177,500. That was acceptable to the vendor. Before entering into a contract to buy, the plaintiffs decided to get a full and detailed survey to ensure that there were going to be no unexpected costs.

(v) Mr Watts instructed the defendant in August 1986. The defendant was asked to provide a full structural survey of the house. Mr Watts told Mrs Morrow, who received the instructions, that he wanted to be sure that the £177,500 offered was the right price in the current market.

(vi) On 26 August the defendant sent to Mr Watts his structural report on the property. The fee charged was £400 plus disbursements and VAT. The report was detailed and long. It mentioned many defects and made recommendations for repairs but the plaintiffs found it reassuring. The general criticism made of the report, which the learned judge held to have been made out, was that, as a recurring theme, the defendant pointed out a defect in the house and then gave a reassurance that the defect could be dealt with as a part of ordinary ongoing maintenance and repair. The "conclusion", which summarized the tone of the report although not all its detail, was as follows:

> "Despite earlier minor settlement I found the overall dwellinghouse to be sound, stable and in good condition. Attention is particularly required to the sometime eradication of wood borer in roofing timbers and to minor works of eradicating continued dampness in ground floor walls. Ideally some insulation would be introduced to upper ceiling areas, but in general, the defects referred to within this report can normally be identified as being associated with regular maintenance required of a building of this age and type.
>
> The foul drainage arrangements, while apparently adequate, and not ideal, some further rationalization and improvement of this may be required in the sometime future, but with attention given to the various aspects referred to within this report, which could well be attended to on an ongoing basis, I am satisfied that a comfortable and largely trouble-free dwelling of considerable charm can be attained."

Nothing was said in the report about the value of the house.

(vii) On receiving the report the plaintiffs read it with care and, as the judge held, reasonably concluded that there was nothing to suggest that any major repairs would be required in the foreseeable future and that nothing was required which could not wait until between them they had funds to spare for such work. Mr Watts by telephone asked the defendant whether the price of £177,500 was fair and whether the repairs which the defendant had recommended would result in substantial expenditure. The defendant replied that the valuation was fair and that no repairs would be substantial in terms of cost. That reply was not relied upon as constituting a warranty, whether express or implied.

(viii) In reliance upon the report the plaintiffs decided to buy the house. The contract was made on 15 October 1986 at the price of £177,500. It was agreed that completion would be deferred and it took place on 10 April 1987 with the assistance of a mortgage loan from Kleinwort Benson to the plaintiffs on ordinary commercial terms.

(ix) Defects were discovered in the house beyond those of which warning was given in the defendant's report. After taking possession in 1987 Mr Watts asked Mr White, a builder, for a quotation for work which included the remedying of certain defects identified by the defendant, namely the roof flashing and defective windows. On examining the house for those purposes, Mr White informed Mr Watts of other defects and Mr Wadey FRICS, was then instructed to carry out a full structural survey. His report, dated 3 August 1987, included the following: (a) that the roof was due for renewal with felting, re-battening and retiling; (b) the chimneys and main walls required repointing in places; (c) lead flashings needed to be installed; (d) window casements and frames generally needed to be upgraded and replaced; (e) the first floor timbers needed specialist woodworm treatment and refixing of firring pieces with extensive renewal of floor boarding. He reported other defects as well which were not relied upon against the defendant at the trial.

(x) If Mrs Watts had known of the defects described in Mr Wadey's report she would not have gone ahead with the purchase. If Mr Watts had known of those defects he would either not have agreed to buy the house or would have agreed to buy only if he had been able to negotiate a substantial reduction in the price based on quotations for the work recommended to roof, to floors and to windows.

(xi) Upon receipt of Mr Wadey's report it was obvious to Mr Watts that building costs running into many thousands of pounds would have to be done urgently. He obtained advice as to his right to claim redress in law for the failure of the defendant to describe the condition of the roof accurately. A formal letter before action was sent. Liability was denied.

(xii) Mr Watts then asked the builder to prepare an estimate for the repairs described in Mr Wadey's report. In September and October Mr White carried out the work to the roof and on 3 November 1987 he was paid £11,212.50 for that work.

(xiii) On 11 November 1987 the writ was issued and in March 1988 the statement of claim was served. The main allegation was that the defendant had negligently failed to observe and advise the plaintiffs that the house was in a defective condition. The loss and damage alleged were, firstly, the difference between the price paid and the value of the house, and, in addition, the cost of repairs, of alternative accommodation, of furniture removal and storage, for loss of use of the property and for the cost in investigation of the defects. There was no allegation of negligent valuation.

(xiv) Between April and October 1988, for a period of six months, the other works, in respect of which claims were made at the trial, were carried out. Because claims in the action were to be made in respect of the work, it was carried out under separate quotations. The times of doing the work and the amounts paid were:

(a) replacing the first floor flooring: £6,840.01: before 20 May 1988;

(b) first floor windows £7,196.70: before 9 July 1988;
(c) exterior brickwork £4,507.42: before 9 September 1988;
(d) flooring: £4,204.72: before 28 October 1988.

Those sums, together with the cost of the roof repairs make up the total of £33,961 awarded as special damages.

(xv) The cost of carrying out those repairs was paid by the plaintiffs by borrowing money. It was the plaintiffs' case that, when the defendant was instructed and made his negligent report, and when the plaintiffs entered into the contract to purchase in October 1986, although the plaintiffs were both high earners, they were "strapped for cash", and hence the importance to them of knowing what the likely financial burdens would be from buying the house. However, between 1986 and 1988 the earned income of both plaintiffs substantially increased. Mrs Watts in 1986 received a salary of £41,000 and a bonus of £6,000 paid in January 1987. Her salary for 1987 was £70,000 and her bonus in January 1988 was £40,000. As to Mr Watts, he earned "very substantially more during 1987 and subsequent years than ... anticipated at the time of purchase". In consequence, the plaintiffs were able to finance the cost not only of the repairs in respect of which the sums listed above were paid but also other repairs (of which the defendant was not said negligently to have failed to inform the plaintiffs) and, in addition, to "decorate and refurbish" the house to a high standard. Mr Watts pointed out that "this process of refurbishment was considerably delayed by the need to undertake the repairs which had neither been foreseen nor budgeted for". The sum expended on all the repairs, decoration and refurbishment was in excess of £150,000.

(xvi) The circumstances which gave rise to the claim for damages for "distress, worry, vexation and inconvenience" were described by Mr Watts as follows:

> "The quality of our life was very seriously affected. We had bought the house on the basis ... that apart from regular maintenance, the property would not require attention. In the event, for eight months we spent almost every weekend staying in a building site. The conditions were quite deplorable. At various times there was scaffolding around the entirety of the house, the first floor boards and the first floor windows were removed in sequence. There was constant dirt and dust permeating the air. Moving our possessions from room to room in accordance with the builder's requirements was a recurrent nightmare and our possessions and furniture became dirty. From time to time there was no internal sanitation and we could not bath. We were forced to spend extended periods out of our first floor bedroom, living and sleeping in the unheated, undecorated attic

rooms. We were most reluctant to entertain our friends and were completely unable to entertain clients.

Throughout the period of building works we continued to spend weekends at the house. As there was no supervising architect or surveyor . . . the only supervision was that provided by me. I believed it to be essential that I spent as much time as possible with the builders to provide them with an incentive to get on with it, to ensure that the work was done to the requisite standard and to provide guidance with the numerous minor problems which arose. I met the builder at the property virtually every weekend.

Our summer holiday in 1988, which we had planned to spend in the house, was spent in an hotel in the Western Isles at an unplanned cost of £880. Both of us were employed in extremely stressful occupations in the city. Weekend relaxation was essential to us both in terms of our physical well-being and our capacity to perform our jobs to the requisite standard. The denial of that relaxation by virtue of the building works caused us both distress. I believe that it was, at the very least, a contributory cause to the unfortunate breakdown of our marriage, which culminated in our separation late in 1989."

The plaintiffs were divorced in April 1990 having separated early in 1989. Mr Watts still owns and occupies the house. Mrs Watts lives in the house in Islington.

(xvii) As to the ground of liability, the judge held that the plaintiffs had reasonably concluded from the defendant's report of August 1986 that no major repairs would be required in the foreseeable future and that nothing was required which could not wait until the two plaintiffs between them had the funds to spare for such work. There was, of course, no finding that the defendant had warranted the absence of any need for major repairs. No such warranty was alleged.

(xviii) As to the difference in value, it was the unchallenged evidence of Mr Wadey, who gave evidence for the plaintiffs at the trial, that in October 1986, the date of the contract to purchase, the value of the house in its true condition was £162,500. It has been common ground in this court that in reliance on the defendant's advice, the plaintiffs paid for the property £15,000 more than the property was worth in its true condition.

The judge's grounds of decision

The judge accepted the evidence of the plaintiffs. As to the measure of damages for the consequences of the negligent advice, the judge accepted that the damages were to be assessed either on the cost of repairs or on the difference in value. He directed himself by reference to the principles stated by Bingham LJ in *County Personnel Ltd* v *Pulver* [1987] 1 WLR 916 at page 925, namely (in brief summary) that the "diminution in value" rule is almost always appropriate where property is acquired following negligent advice by surveyors; but that that is not an invariable approach and should not be mechanistically applied in cases where it may appear inappropriate. He observed that the circumstances of the present case were remarkably similar to the facts in *Syrett* v *Carr & Neave* (see page 121 in this volume) a case also decided by him. The learned judge then, after reference to the receipt by the plaintiffs of Mr Wadey's report on 3 August 1987, stated the ground of his decision in accordance with his reasoning in *Syrett* as follows:

> "If the plaintiffs had then sought to cut their losses by reselling, they would have incurred very considerable costs in reselling (in the shape of agent's and solicitor's fees and stamp duty) and in finding a new property if that had been their chosen course of action. In addition, they might have incurred a very substantial loss on the resale in very different market conditions when they were selling what would have become a suspect house, and they would have had to devote much time to the sale of the house. In the very difficult position in which they found themselves, I find that they acted entirely reasonably in deciding to repair the premises rather than resell."

He therefore held that the plaintiffs were entitled to recover damages assessed as the cost of repair of the premises as to those items of which complaint had been made, namely £33,961.35. It is to be noted that there was nothing in the plaintiffs' pleaded case as to what costs they would have incurred upon reselling.

As to the claim for general damages for distress and inconvenience the judge rejected the submission for the defendants, based upon *Hayes* v *Dodd* [1990] 2 All ER 815 that such damages are not recoverable in this class of case. That case, he held, did illustrate features for which damages of that sort should not be awarded. He noted the reference to the physical consequences of the breach of duty as justifying an award in the judgment of Kerr LJ. As a matter of policy, in his view, damages for mental distress in contract are limited to certain classes of case including "... where the contract which has been broken was itself a contract to provide peace of mind or freedom from distress ...": see *per* Dillon LJ in *Bliss* v *South East Thames RHA* [1987] ICR 700 at 718. The judge held that, on the authorities cited, in appropriate circumstances a negligent surveyor of a residential property, which he has undertaken to survey for a prospective purchaser of the property who intends to live there, may be liable to his client in damages to compensate him or her for inconvenience and distress arising out of living in the property but not out of litigation about it. The judge commented that a prospective buyer of a house goes to a surveyor not just to be advised on the financial advisability of one of the most important transactions of his life but also to receive re-assurance that when he buys the house he will have "peace of mind and freedom from distress".

As to the amount of damages, they should be on a scale which is not excessive but modest: see *per* Lord Denning MR in *Perry* v *Sidney Phillips* [1982] 1 WLR 1297 at pages 1302, 1303; 22 BLR 120. The judge then set out the description of the distress and inconvenience which the plaintiffs suffered in the house, limited to weekends, in the terms set out in the proof of Mr Watts repeated in paragraph (xvi) *above.* The judge declined to allow the £880, the cost of the holiday in 1988, as special damages but held that it was to be taken into account in assessing general damages for distress and inconvenience. He rejected the contention that, since the plaintiffs had voluntarily undertaken works going far beyond the works the subject of the action, therefore their alleged distress and inconvenience should be discounted. The answer of Mr Watts had been that, once it became necessary to do certain works, other works naturally followed: for example, once the floor had to come up it was only natural and sensible that the wiring and under-floor plumbing also should be dealt with, even though those matters would not normally have been considered for some years. The judge held that answer of Mr Watts to be sensible and well founded. The judge also considered, although the point had not been argued for the plaintiffs, whether the breakdown of the plaintiffs' marriage could be taken into account and held that, as a matter of policy, it could not be. The judge then held that the totality of the distress and inconvenience, assessed on a modest scale, should be set at £4,000 for each plaintiff.

As to interest, the judge was invited by counsel for the plaintiffs to allow interest at 15% on the award in respect of damages based on the cost of repairs. The contention for the defendant was that interest should be at the short-term interest account rates. Judge Bowsher, without giving any detailed reasons, held that the appropriate rate of interest was 15% on the £33.961.35 calculated from the dates of payment by the plaintiffs and 2% on general damages.

The contest on the main issue: diminution in value or cost of repairs?

Before describing the submissions which have been made on this appeal it is necessary to refer to the decisions of this court in *Phillips* v *Ward* [1956] 1 WLR 471; 4 BLR 142 and *Perry* v *Sidney Phillips* [1982] 1 WLR 1297; 22 BLR 120 to which detailed reference has been made in the submissions of counsel. In *Phillips* the plaintiff, in reliance upon a negligent report by a surveyor, purchased in June 1952 for £25,00 an Elizabethan manor house farm consisting of house, two cottages, and some land. The surveyor failed to report that the timbers of the house were badly affected by death watch beetle and worm so that the only course was to replace the roof by a new roof and to rebuild the timbers, etc. The market value of the property in its actual condition was £21,000. After moving into the house with his family the plaintiff found that it would require an additional expenditure of £7,000 at 1952 prices to put the property into the condition in which it had been described in the report. The plaintiff clamed, among other heads of claim, the cost of repairs ruling at the date of trial. The official referee awarded £4,000, namely the difference between the value of the property as it should have been described and its value as described. This court (Denning, Morris and Romer LJJ) held that the proper measure of damages was the difference in money between the value of the property in the condition described and its value as it should have been described, namely £4,000. It is necessary to set out some passages in the judgments. It has been common ground on this appeal that the diminution in value rule is more accurately to be expressed as the difference between the price paid and the value in its true description at least where no point is taken, as in this case, that the plaintiff chose to pay above market value.

Denning LJ at page 473 said:

> "I take it to be clear law that the proper measure of damages is the amount of money which will put the plaintiff into as good a position as if the surveying contract had been properly fulfilled: see *British Westinghouse Electric and Manufacturing Co Ltd* v *Underground Electric Railways Co* [1912] AC 673, 689: *per* Lord Haldane LC. Now if [the surveyor] had carried out his contract, he would have reported the bad state of the timbers. On receiving that report, Mr Phillips would either have refused to have anything to do with the house — in which case he would have suffered no damage — or he would have bought it for a sum which represented its fair value in its bad condition — in which case he would pay so much less on that account. The proper measure of damages is therefore the difference between the value in its assumed good condition and the value in the bad condition which should have been reported to the client.
>
> We were referred to the cases where the house is damaged or destroyed by the fault of a tortfeasor. These cases are, I think, different. If the injured person reasonably goes to the expense of repairing the house, the tortfeasor may well be bound to pay the cost of repair, less an allowance because new work takes the place of old: see *Lukin* v *Godsall* [1795] Peake Add Cas 15 and *Hide* v *Thornborough* [1846] 2 Car & Kir 250. In other cases, the tortfeasor may only have to pay the value of the house: see *Moss* v *Christchurch RDC*

> [1925] 2 KB 750. It all depends on the circumstances of the case: see *Murphy* v *Wexford CC* [1921] IR 230. The general rule is that the injured person is to be fairly compensated for the damage he has sustained, neither more nor less."

Later in his judgment at page 474 Denning LJ said:

> "So also in this action, if Mr Phillips were to recover from the surveyor the sum of £7,000, it would mean that Mr Phillips would get for £18,000 (£25,000 paid less £7,000 received) a house and land which were worth £21,000. That cannot be right. The proper amount for him to recover is £4,000."

Morris LJ at page 475 said:

> "In my judgment, the damages to be assessed were such as could fairly and reasonably be considered as resulting naturally from the failure of the defendant to report as he should have done ... It is said ... that (the official referee) was not warranted in proceeding on the basis ... of the difference between the value of the property as it was described in the defendant's report and its value as it should have been described. In my view, however, that was the correct basis on the facts of this case."

Romer LJ, after giving the same reasons for holding that the diminution in value was the correct measure of damages, said at page 478:

> "It may well be that if, on learning of the real condition of the house, he had decided to leave and resell, he would have been entitled to recover from the defendant, in addition to the £4,000, his costs and expenses of moving in and moving out and of the resale. As, however, he elected to stay, after all the facts had become known to him, this point does not arise."

In the case of *Perry* in 1982 the surveyor failed to observe serious defects including a leaking roof and a septic tank with an offensive smell. The plaintiff could not afford major repairs and executed only minor repairs himself. At the date of the trial the plaintiff was still occupying the house as his home. The judge awarded damages assessed in respect of repairing the defects as at the date of trial in 1981. Between the date of the trial and the hearing of the appeal the plaintiff sold the property for £43,000. He had paid £27,000 in 1976 in reliance upon the negligent report. It was acknowledged by the plaintiff that sale of the house without repairs having been executed made it difficult to support the award based upon the cost of repairs and his contention was that damages should be assessed on the basis of the difference in market value of the property as between its value taking into account the defects for which the judge found liability established and its value in the condition the defendants reported it to be either on the basis of values at the date of the report or at the date of judgment.

Lord Denning at page 1301, after reference to the measure of damages for breach of contract to build a house, or to do repairs to it, or in respect of damages done to it (*Dodd Properties (Kent) Ltd* v *Canterbury CC* [1981] WLR 433, continued:

> "Where there is a contract by a prospective buyer with a surveyor under which the surveyor agrees to survey a house and make a report on it — and he makes it negligently — and the client buys the house on the faith of the report, then the damages are to be assessed at the time of the breach, according to the difference in price which the buyer would have given if the report had been carefully made from that which he in fact gave owing to the negligence of the surveyor. The surveyor gives no warranty that there are no defects other than those in his report. There is no question of specific performance. The conract has already been performed, albeit negligently. The buyer is not entitled to remedy the defects and charge the cost to the surveyor. He is only entitled to damages for the breach of contract or for negligence. It was so decided by this court in *Phillips* v *Ward* [1956] 1 WLR 471, followed in *Simple Simon Catering Ltd* v *Binstock Miller & Co* (1973) 117 SJ 529."

Oliver LJ at page 1304C said:

> "The position as I see it is simply this, that the plaintiff has been misled by a negligent survey report into paying more for the property than that property was actually worth. The position, as I see it, is exactly the same as that which arose in *Phillips* v *Ward* . . . and in the subsequent case of *Ford* v *White & Co* [1964] 1 WLR 885 . . ."

At page 1304F Oliver LJ continued:

> "I see nothing . . . which justifies the proposition . . . that damages are to be assessed on the basis of some hypothetical value at the date of the trial because the plaintiff has chosen — as he did in this case — to retain the property and not to cut his loss by reselling it . . . the right measure of damage is the measure suggested in both *Phillips* v *Ward* and *Ford* v *White & Co* which is simply the difference between what the plaintiff paid for the property and its value at the date when he obtained it."

Kerr LJ at page 1306 reserved his view as to whether in a case like this the approach by way of cost of repairs is necessarily right since the point had not been argued.

Mr Jackson, in support of the contention that the judge was wrong in law in failing to apply the diminution in value rule, submitted that this case on the facts cannot be validly distinguished from, and should therefore be decided in accordance with, the decision of this court in *Phillips* by awarding no more than the sum of £15,000, together with interest. *Phillips* was, he submitted a decision in which, upon analysis of the ordinary relationship between the purchaser of a dwellinghouse and the surveyor advising him as to the condition of that house, this court was applying, and not failing to apply, what has been called the "over-riding rule" of restitution in relation to damages, that is as stated by Lord Blackburn in *Livingstone* v *Rawyards Coal Co*, or as stated by Lord Haldane LC in *British Westinghouse Electric Co Ltd*, to which Denning LJ referred in his judgment in *Phillips*. That was recognized by this court in *County Personnel* v *Pulver* where, in a passage cited by Judge Bowsher in his judgment in this case, Bingham LJ said, after reference to the over-riding rule of restitution, at page 925F:

> "On the authorities as they stand the diminution in value rule appears almost always, if not always, to be appropriate where property is acquired following negligent advice by surveyors. Such cases as *Phillips* v *Ward* [1956] 1 WLR 471; *Pilkington* v *Wood* [1953] Ch 770; *Ford* v *White & Co* [1964] 1 WLR 885 and *Perry* v *Sidney Phillips & Son* [1982] 1 WLR 1297, lay down that rule ..."

In commenting upon the judge's findings of fact with reference to the plaintiffs' decision not to resell but to carry out repairs, Mr Jackson submitted that, since on the plaintiffs' expert evidence the value of the house in its true condition in August 1987 was £185,000 (£7,500 more than the plaintiffs had paid in April 1987), the plaintiffs could have sold, have paid the sums wasted on fees, etc, and have been in the same financial position in August 1987 as immediately before exchange of contracts. This point was made, as I understood the argument, not in order to justify application of the diminution in value rule (which was submitted to be correctly applied irrespective of the financial consequences on resale), nor to criticise the finding that it was reasonable for the plaintiffs not to resell — (it was conceded that it was reasonable if the plaintiffs wished so to act for their own purposes) — but to demonstrate the consequences of the application of the rule to either course of conduct which the plaintiffs might have chosen to follow.

Mr Jackson drew to the court's attention a large number of cases decided since *Phillips* in which the diminution in value rule had been applied. He submitted that in those cases where the diminution in value rule had not been applied, and where there was no justification on the facts for not applying it, the decisions were wrong, including, in his submission, *Hipkins* v *Cotton* [1989] 2 EGLR 157, Scott Baker J, and *Syrett* v *Carr & Neave* (see page 121 below) Judge Bowsher.

For the plaintiffs, Mr Naughton submitted that the judge was right in his conclusion for the reasons given by him. The judge had correctly applied the over-riding rule of restitution. This court, it was said, in *Phillips* had not laid down any particular rule which the judge was required to follow so as to prevent application of that over-riding rule: he referred to *The Chekiang* [1926] AC 637 and to the *SS Susquehanna* [1926] AC 655 for support for the proposition that a rule cannot be laid down which will apply to the measure of damages in cases of a particular category if application of the rule in a particular case in that category will result in departing from the rule of restitution.

The substance of Mr Naughton's submission on the facts of this case was that the plaintiffs had bought the house in reliance upon the report of the defendant as to its condition; the house was not in the condition described; in consequence the plaintiffs spent £33,961 to put the house in the condition in which, on reading the defendant's report, they believed the house to be; and, therefore, if the damages be limited to £15,000, in accordance with the diminution in value rule, the over-riding rule of restitution is not satisfied.

Mr Naughton was willing to concede that the principle in *Phillips*, in so far as it can be regarded as a prima facie rule for the measure of damages in a claim against a negligent surveyor, is applicable in, but, he said, only in, a case where it is clear that the plaintiffs would have bought the house any way, ie even if it had been accurately described by the surveyor. He referred to and relied upon *Hayes* v *Dodd* [1990] 2 All ER 815, a case of negligent advice by solicitors as to the existence of a necessary right of way for the use of land for a motor repair business by the clients who bought that land. Properly advised, the clients would not have bought the premises. Staughton LJ referred to such a case as a "no transaction case" and contrasted it with a case where the claimant would still have bought the property if he had been correctly advised as to its condition which he referred to as a "successful transaction" case. In that case, the plaintiffs recovered damages on the basis that it was a "no transaction" case and damages were awarded in the amount of the capital expenditure thrown away in the purchase of the business and the expenses incurred in extricating themselves from the purchase. He relied also on *Steward* v *Rapley* [1989] 1 EGLR 159 where, he submitted, in a claim against a negligent surveyor, Staughton LJ again held that in a "no transaction" case, the cost of repairs as contrasted with the diminution in value, may be the appropriate measure of damage.

Mr Naughton made detailed submissions designed to show that, if these plaintiffs, on discovering the defects missed by the defendant, had decided to sell the house, the damages which they would have suffered, and which would have been recoverable from the defendant, would have been substantial and probably greater than the £33,961, the cost of repairs. In outline, those damages, it was said, would have included at least £8,733 for agent's commission and solicitor's fees on resale; removal costs; solicitor's fees and stamp duty on a replacement purchase; the loss on resale which would have been £17,250; the costs of seeking an alternative property; the increase in cost of the replacement house in the sum of at least £25,800, being 15% on £172,000; and the wasted cost of borrowing the purchase price of the house which Mr Naughton put at £1,000 per month from completion in April 1987 until resale at earliest some months after August 1987 when Mr Wadey's report was received. The points made by reference to these potential losses on resale were, as I understood the argument, primarily intended to answer the submission made by Mr Jackson; and, then, firstly to show that the award of the cost of repairs at £33,900 is thus shown to be moderate and not excessive; secondly, that the nature and extent of such damages upon resale had been left out of account in the reasons given by the members of this court in *Phillips*; and, thirdly, by demonstrating the unreality of any suggestion that the plaintiffs could sensibly have chosen to sell the house instead of deciding to repair it, to make good the judge's ruling that the plaintiffs are entitled to recover the cost of repairs because, as in *Syrett*, the plaintiffs had had no real opportunity of cutting their losses by reselling.

I have given no more than a brief summary of Mr Naughton's argument in which he referred to a number of cases and to the comments made in text books. The argument followed the reasoning in Judge Bowsher's judgment in *Syrett* and the suggestion made in *Professional Negligence*, Dugdale and Stanton, 2 Edn, 1988, paragraph 20.34, where it was submitted that if, being correctly advised, the plaintiff would have withdrawn, the natural measure of his loss is to indemnify him against the losses incurred as a result of acquiring the property; that the correct measure of damage, despite the decision in *Phillips*, is the cost of repair provided that it is "reasonable for him to retain the property and to incur the cost of repairs"; and that such an award does not "amount to a surveyor warranting the quality of the building, it merely reflects the losses which the plaintiff incurs and needs to be indemnified against".

The reasoning of Judge Bowsher in *Syrett*'s case, and the argument based upon the alleged potential unfairness of the application of the diminution in value rule, particularly in cases of the purchase of dwellinghouses by purchasers of limited means, makes it necessary to try to test the ruling in *Phillips* by reference to basic principles in a variety of possible situations.

In the end, I have reached the conclusion that the defendant is right in his contentions on this issue and that, on the facts of this case, the financial loss of the plaintiffs is in law limited to the diminution in value of £15,000 with interest therein. My reasons are as follows.

The task of the court is to award to the plaintiffs that sum of money which will, so far as possible, put the plaintiff into as good a position as if the contract for the survey had been properly fulfilled: see Denning LJ in *Phillips*. It is important to note that the contract in this case, as in *Phillips*, was the usual contract for the survey of a house for occupation with no special terms beyond the undertaking of the surveyor to use proper care and skill in reporting upon the condition of the house.

The decision in *Phillips* case was based upon that principle: in particular, if the contract had been properly performed the plaintiff either would not have bought, in which case he would have avoided any loss, or, after negotiation, he would have paid the reduced price. In the absence of evidence to show that any other or additional recoverable benefit would have been obtained as a result of proper performance, the price will be taken to have been reduced to the market price of the house in its true condition because it cannot be assumed that the vendor would have taken less.

The cost of doing repairs to put right defects negligently not reported may be relevant to the proof of the market price of the house in its true condition: see *Steward* v *Rapley* [1989] 1 EGLR 159; and the cost of doing repairs and the diminution in value may be shown to be the same. If, however, the cost of repairs would exceed the diminution in value, then the ruling in *Phillips*, where it is applicable, prohibits recovery of the excess because it would give to the plaintiff more than his loss. It would put the plaintiff in the position of recovering damages for breach of a warranty that the condition of the house was correctly described by the surveyor and, in the ordinary case as here, no such warranty has been given.

It is clear, and it was not argued to the contrary, that the ruling in *Phillips* may be applicable to the case where the buyer has, after purchase, extricated himself from the transaction by selling the property. In the absence of any point on mitigation, the buyer will recover the diminution in value together with costs and expenses thrown away in moving in and out and of resale: see Romer LJ in

Phillips. I will not here try to state the nature or extent of any additional recoverable items of damage.

The damages recoverable where the plaintiff extricates himself from the transaction by resale are not necessarily limited to the diminution in value plus expenses. The consequences of the negligent advice and of the plaintiff entering into the transaction into which he would not have entered if properly advised, may be such that the diminution in value rule is not applicable. An example is the case of *County Personnel* v *Pulver* [1987] 1 WLR 916, a case of solicitors' negligence, where the plaintiff recovered the capital losses caused by entering into the transaction.

It is also clear, and again there was no argument for the plaintiffs to the contrary, that, if the plaintiff would have bought the house anyway, if correctly advised, the ruling in *Phillips* is applicable: the fact that after purchase he discovers that the unreported defects will cost more than the diminution in value does not entitle him to recover the excess. That is, again, because, if the contract had been performed properly, he would have negotiated and, absent proof of a different outcome, would have done no better than reduction to the market value in true condition.

It was rightly acknowledged for the plaintiffs that proof that the plaintiff, properly advised, would not have bought the property does not by itself cause the diminution in value role to be inapplicable. It was contended, however, that it becomes inapplicable if it is also proved that it is reasonable for the plaintiff to retain the property and to do the repairs. I cannot accept that submission because:

(i) the fact that it is reasonable for the plaintiff to retain the property and to do the repairs seems to me to be irrelevant to determination of the question whether recovery of the cost of repairs is justified in order to put the plaintiff in the position in which he would have been if the contract, ie the promise to make a careful report, had been performed. The position is no different from that in *Phillips*: the plaintiff would either have refused to buy or he would have negotiated a reduced price. Recovery of the cost of repairs after having gone into possession: that is to say in effect the acquisition of the house at the price paid less the cost of repairs at the later date of doing those repairs, is not a position into which the plaintiff could have been put as a result of proper performance of the contract. Nor is that cost recoverable as damages for breach of any promise by the defendant because, as stated above, there was no promise that the plaintiff would not incur any such cost.

(ii) In the context of the contract proved in this case, I have difficulty in seeing when or by reference to what principle it would not be reasonable for the purchaser of a house to retain it and to do the repairs. He is free to do as he pleases. He can owe no duty to the surveyor to take any cheaper course. The measure of damages should depend, and in my view does depend, upon proof of the sum needed to put the plaintiff in the position in which he would have been if the contract was properly performed, and a reasonable decision by him to remain in the house and to repair it, upon discovery of the defects, cannot alter that primary sum which remains the amount by which he was caused to pay more than the value of the house in its true condition.

(iii) If the rule were as contended for by the plaintiffs, what limit, if any, could be put on the nature and extent of the repairs of which the plaintiff could recover the cost? Mr Naughton asserted that the cost of repairs awarded in this case was no more than putting the house in the condition in which, on reading the report, they believed the house to be. That, however, contains no relevant standard of reasonableness because, again, the defendant did not warrant that description to be true. To argue that to award damages on that basis is not to enforce a warranty never given but merely to "reflect the losses which the plaintiffs have incurred" seems to me to be a circular statement.

(iv) I have considered whether the reasonableness of the amount which a plaintiff might recover towards the cost of repairing unreported defects in excess of the diminution in value might be determined by reference to the amount which the plaintiff could recover if he sold the property: ie the diminution in value plus any other recoverable losses and expenses. Such a limit was not contended for by Mr Naughton. It has the apparent attraction of enabling a plaintiff who chooses to retain the property to recover as much as he would recover if he chose to sell it. It seems to me, however, to be impossible to hold that such is the law in the case of such a contract as was made in this case. The plaintiff must, I think, prove that the loss which he claims to have suffered was caused by the breach of duty proved and he cannot do that by proving what his loss would have been in circumstances which have not happened.

It is necessary to test the conclusion which I have reached as set out above by examining the cases of *Hipkins* and *Syrett* which Mr Jackson submitted were wrongly decided.

In *Hipkins* Scott Baker J held that application of the diminution in value rule would manifestly not do justice in that particular case. On applying that rule the damages would have been £8,900 with interest from the summer of 1981. The cost of repairs which the plaintiff was held reasonably to have carried out in 1985, after advice in 1982 to "wait and see", was £14,211. I accept that, if I am right in the conclusion which I have described above, there is no valid ground of distinction reported in *Hipkins* and that, therefore, the award on the facts found should have been £8,900 with interest.

Next, in *Syrett*, the reasoning of Judge Bowsher may be summarized, I think, as follows. He held that it was to be inferred that in *Phillips* the purchaser, on discovering the defect on moving in, had the choice between selling the property at its true value, making the loss which was less than the then cost of repairs, or of doing the repairs. To award in those circumstances the cost of doing the repairs would have been to give him a benefit to which he was not entitled in the absence of a warranty from the surveyor as to the state of the property. There was, however, no such giving of a benefit to which the plaintiff was not entitled on the facts in *Syrett*, because instant resale would not, at that date, have left the purchaser with a loss less than the cost of repairs and, more importantly, the purchaser had no reason to make an instant sale of the property because she did not know of the defect until two years after moving in. Similarly in *Perry*, the unreported defects were discovered soon after moving in and, in that case also, the plaintiff had a choice of either cutting his loss by reselling or of undertaking the necessary repairs. Since, however, the plaintiff in *Syrett* was unaware of the unreported defects until two years after the purchase, she was entitled to the cost of repairs because she had not had an opportunity of cutting her losses about the date of purchase and had acted reasonably throughout.

With respect to the learned judge, I do not find that reasoning to be convincing and, in my view, the decision in *Syrett* was wrong. It is true that both in *Phillips* and in *Perry* the plaintiff on discovering the unreported defects, had the choice of selling or undertaking the necessary repairs. This court held that, whichever choice was made, the primary sum for damages was the diminution in value together with any expenses, etc, caused by the breach. There is, however, nothing to suggest that it was the existence of that choice or opportunity at any particular time which caused the proper measure of damages to be stated as the diminution in value. Since that statement was expressly explained by reference to putting the plaintiff in the position in which he would have been if the contract had been properly performed, and since that concept is not affected by the subsequent date of discovery of breach, the fact that in *Syrett* the claimant did not discover the breach until two years after purchase seems to me to be irrelevant to the measure of damages as based upon the diminution in value. I would, however, reserve with reference to this point the question as to the date at which the diminution in value is to be calculated. Upon discovering the breach the plaintiff can decide whether on that ground to sell. In *Phillips*, the measure of damages was stated by Morris LJ as the difference between the value of the property as it was described in the negligent report and its value as it should have been described in 1952. If the unreported defects had been discovered three years later, and if the value of the property in either state had increased by 25% as a result of inflation of house prices, it seems to me to be arguable that this measure of damage should be taken as the difference between the values so increased: ie £5,000, being £31,250 less £26,250. No such point was raised in this case.

Next, as to the grounds of decision in *Syrett*, if (in the case of the ordinary contract) an award of the cost of repairs to a plaintiff who discovers the defects on moving in is to give to him a benefit to which he is not entitled (and I agree that it is — see *Phillips*), it is no less the giving of a benefit to which the plaintiff is not entitled to award him the cost of repairs when he discovers the defects years after moving in: the principle that an award of the cost of repairs is a benefit to which the plaintiff is not entitled depends upon the terms of the contract between the plaintiff and the surveyor and not upon the time of discovery of the unreported defects.

Lastly, in *Syrett*, the opportunity to "cut losses" at about the date of sale, which it was held was denied to the claimant in *Syrett*, is, as I understand it, the opportunity to decide to sell and to suffer the loss of the diminution in value which would be recoverable. If the plaintiff decided instead to do the repairs he would incur any additional cost over this diminution in value as a result of his own decision; but, if he did not discover the defects until two years later, having been deprived of that earlier opportunity, he becomes, it is said, entitled to the full cost of repairs and not, be it noted, only the amount by which the cost of repairs may be shown to have increased since the date of purchase. As I have said above, however, the opportunity to sell on discovery of the defects was not the reason for holding in *Phillips* that the measure of damages was the diminution in value: that holding resulted from the application of the basic principle of restitution to the terms of the contract between the claimant and the surveyor. Delay in discovery of the defects does not affect that application of that principle. A decision to remain and to carry out repairs after such delayed discovery cannot, in my judgment, alter the proper measure of damages.

One further matter must, I think, be examined. It is, I think, clear law that where a claimant is caused to enter into a transaction in consequence of negligent advice, as in the case of a surveyor employed under the ordinary contract, the claimant may be entitled to all the losses incurred as a result of entering into the transaction where he would not have entered into the transaction if properly advised and the losses are caused by entry into the transaction and by extrication from it. An example in the case of a solicitor's advice is, as I have mentioned above, *County Personnel* v *Pulver*. Can the claim of these plaintiffs to the cost of repairs properly be put on the same basis: ie as damages caused by entering into a transaction in reliance on the bad advice, and, if not, why not? On this part of the argument, Mr Naughton referred to a number of matters and, in particular, to the fact that it is in many cases unrealistic to measure the damages of the purchaser by reference to the value of the property where it is not his intention to resell the house but to live in it and resale is impossible for means unconnected with value in the market. If the buyer is caused to buy a house by a negligent report which does not warn him of the existence of defects, and which he must cause to be repaired in order to live in the house in the condition in which he expected it to be, why is not the cost of repairs a loss resulting from entering into the transaction just as much as the payments recovered in the case of *County Personnel* v *Pulver*? Since such a buyer has no intention of selling — he is repairing his home not an article of commerce — any addition to the value of the house, it was said, will not be at once realized and he is not in truth thereby getting any advantage beyond what he reasonably thought he was getting when he relied upon the surveyor's advice.

I recognize the force of these points so far as concerns the position of such an unfortunate claimant. From his point of view, it would, indeed, be better if the surveyor could be treated as having warranted that no repairs beyond those described as indicated in the survey report, would be required within some period of time. No such warranty, however, was given in this case, or said to have been given, and, in the absence of such a warranty, there is no basis for awarding the cost of repairs.

I would, therefore, hold that the judgment for £33,961, the cost of repairs, must be set aside and that, in substitution therefore, judgment should be entered for financial loss in the sum of £15,000 with interest at 15% from the date of payment until judgment: I understand it to be common ground that payment is to be taken as having been made as to £1,500, from the date of payment of the deposit of £17,750 on the making of the contract, and as to the balance of £13,500 at the date of completion, based upon the proportion of the excess payment of £15,000 to the total sum agreed to be paid. If I am wrong in my understanding I would wish to hear counsel upon that matter. I shall deal later in this judgment with my reasons for confirming the rate of interest at 15% as awarded by the judge.

General damages: the award for "distress and inconvenience".

For the defendant, Mr Jackson submitted that, on the facts of this case, the plaintiffs were entitled to no award under this head but that, if any sum was due, the award was plainly excessive and far greater than sums commonly awarded, in accordance with *Perry,* as "modest" compensation. His contention was that, in a contract of this nature, general damages are not recoverable for mere mental distress; and are recoverable only for the enduring of physical discomfort and inconvenience in the measuring of which regard may properly be had to the mental reaction to such physical discomfort. He further criticized the judge's conclusion on this part of the case on the ground that the judge did not make any finding as to the nature or extent of any physical discomfort which had been caused by the defendant's breach of contract as contrasted with physical discomfort caused by the plaintiffs' decision to carry out substantial additional repairs and refurbishment.

Mr Naughton submitted that it was decided by the decision of this court in *Perry* that damages for mental distress can be recovered against a negligent surveyor in the ordinary case and that such a contract is in the same category as contracts for the provision of holiday: see *Jarvis* v *Swan's Tours* [1973] 1 QB 233 and *Jackson* v *Horizon Holidays* [1975] 1 WLR 1468. The misery and discomfort experienced by the claimants in the position of these plaintiffs is not, he said, linked to the cost of the works carried out or to the time taken to complete them. The hardship should be seen as subjective and that is best assessed by the judge who heard the evidence. The fact that this was the second home for hard-working and stressed individuals should be seen as increasing the proper compensation and not as reducing it. Further, the fact that the house was expensive, and that the use of it for relaxation could be regarded as costing the interest on the price paid, would justify a larger award in comparison with an award in respect of a cheaper house.

As to the law, it is, in my judgment, clear that the plaintiffs were not entitled to recover general damages for mental distress not caused by physical discomfort or inconvenience resulting from the breach of contract. It is true that in *Perry* Lord Denning justified the award of damages for anxiety, worry and distress (ie "modest compensation") by reference to the holiday cases of *Jarvis* and *Jackson* and to *Heywood* v *Wellers* [1976] QB 446, a solicitor's case. I do not, however, accept that *Perry* is authority for that proposition. It is, I think, clear that, in that case, the award of damages (which was upheld) was for "vexation, that is the discomfort and so on suffered by the plaintiff as a result of having to live for a lengthy period in a defective house which for one reason or another was not repaired over the period between the acquisition by the plaintiff and the date of the trial": see *per* Oliver LJ page 1304 H. Further, in *Perry* Kerr LJ at page 1307 said:

> "It should be noted that the judge has awarded these (damages for vexation and inconvenience) not for the tension or frustration of a person who is involved in a legal dispute in which the other party refuses to meet its liabilities. If he had done so, it would have been wrong, because such aggravation is experienced by almost all litigants. He has awarded these damages because of the physical consequences of the breach which were all forceable at the time . . ."

Mr Jackson's submission is, I think, correct. In *Bailey* v *Bullock* [1950] 2 All ER 1162, Barry J, in a case of solicitor's negligence, held that damages for inconvenience and discomfort could be recovered for the solicitor's failure to get possession of premises for his client but not damages for annoyance and mental distress. So holding he relied upon the judgment of Scott LJ in *Groom* v *Crocker* [1939] 1 KB 194 at 224 where *Addis* v *Gramophone Co Ltd* [1909] AC 488 was held to be a conclusive authority against general damages for injury to reputation or feelings. Barry J contrasted that decision with that of *Hobbs* v *London & South Western Railway* (1875) LR 10 QB 111 where damages for physical inconvenience were upheld for breach of a contract of carriage.

In *Jarvis,* it was held that the old authorities excluding damages for disappointment of mind were out of date and that damages for mental distress can be recovered in contract in a proper case. One such proper case was held there to be breach of a contract for a holiday or of a contract to provide entertainment and enjoyment. Breach of a contract of carriage, where vexation may be caused, was distinguished from breach of a contract for a holiday where the provision of pleasure is promised.

Again, in *Heywood* v *Wellers* [1976] QB 446, damages were awarded against a negligent solicitor for failure to obtain protection from his client against molestation, and in particular for the client's distress, because the solicitors were employed to protect the client from molestation which was causing distress. In *Hayes* v *Dodd* [1990] 2 All ER 818 Purchas LJ at page 826, with reference to a claim to damages for mental distress in a claim against a surveyor, said:

> "I agree with the approach adopted by Staughton LJ reflecting, as it does, the judgment of Dillon LJ in *Bliss* v *South East Thames Regional Health Authority* [1987] 1 ICR 700 at 718, namely that damages of this kind are only recoverable when the subject matter of the contract or duty in tort is to provide peace of mind or freedom from distress."

If, then, the plaintiffs, for breach of a contract of this nature, are entitled only to damages in respect of physical discomfort or inconvenience resulting from the breach, it is clear, as in *Perry,* that such damages are recoverable where, as contemplated by the defendant, the plaintiffs move into the property and live there in physical discomfort because of the existence of unreported defects such as an evil-smelling cesspit or a leaking roof. But what of physical discomfort caused not by the defects but by the process of repairing them in a case where, as here, the surveyor has not warranted that there are no defects? Thus, in this case, there was no discomfort caused by any defect in the roof: it was replaced before it leaked or collapsed. Mr Jackson, rightly, I think, did not contend that damages for physical discomfort are not recoverable where caused by the carrying out of repairs to negligently-unreported defects even though the surveyor is not in law liable for the cost of those repairs. The concession seems to me to be rightly made provided it is shown that the parties contemplated that, upon the plaintiff occupying the house at his home in reliance upon the report, he would in fact have to live there while the repairs are done and it is reasonable for him to do so. We do not have to decide whether, if the plaintiff has to rent other accommodation during the carrying out of repairs, such costs will be recoverable in the absence of any contractual warranty as to the existence of defects requiring repairs, and I would reserve my decision upon it.

In his judgment, Judge Bowsher, after reference to *Hayes* v *Dodd*, and to *Perry* held that a negligent surveyor of a residential property, which he has undertaken to survey for a prospective purchaser who intends to live there, may be liable to his client in damages to compensate him for "inconvenience and distress arising out of living in the property but not out of litigation about it". Judge Bowsher continued that that seemed to him to be the case whether the position be rationalized by reference to "special relationship" or "a contract to provide peace of mind or freedom from distress". A prospective buyer of a house goes to a surveyor, said Judge Bowsher, not just to be advised on the financial advisability of one of the most important transactions of his life but also to receive reassurance that, when he buys the house, he will have "peace of mind and freedom from distress".

It is clear, I think, that the judge was regarding the contract between these plaintiffs and the defendant as a contract in which the subject matter was to provide peace of mind or freedom from distress within the meaning of Dillon LJ's phrase in *Bliss* cited by Purchas LJ in *Hayes* v *Dodd.* That, with respect, seems to me to be an impossible view of the ordinary surveyor's contract. No doubt house buyers hope to enjoy peace of mind and freedom from distress as a consequence of the proper performance by a surveyor of his contractual obligation to provide a careful report, but there was no express promise for the provision of peace of mind or freedom from distress and no such implied promise was alleged. In my view, in the case of the ordinary surveyor's contract, damages are only recoverable for distress caused by physical consequences of the breach of contract. Since the judge did not attempt to assess the award on that basis this court must reconsider the award and determine what it should be.

For my part, I accept that the award was excessive even if the judge had directed himself correctly. It was very substantially more than the awards made in similar cases apart from the award by the same judge in *Syrett.* The other cases to which we were referred for this purpose included the following and I have listed the amount of the award together with the amount adjusted for inflation since the date of the award: *Roberts* v *Hampton* [1989] 2 All ER 504: £1,500 (£1,890); *Cross* v *Martin* [1989] 1 EGLR 159: £1,000 (£1,260); *Steward* v *Rapley* [1989] 1 EGLR 159: £2,000 (£2,520); *Bigg* v *Howard* [1990] 1 EGLR 173: £1,600 (£1,744); *Hipkins* v *Cotton* [1989] 2 EGLR 157: £750 (£877). In the first three cases the award stated was to two plaintiffs. In each case the award was in respect of a period of inconvenience and discomfort in the claimants' home.

The judge accepted the evidence of the plaintiffs in full. The period of physical discomfort caused by the carrying out of work extended over eight months. It started in September 1987 when work to the roof began and was completed in October. The time taken in performing that work is not more exactly proved. Scaffolding was around the house. Work in respect of unreported defects began again in 1988 and was done under separate quotations before the several dates stated in paragraph (xiv) *above* ending in October 1988. The periods of physical discomfort were limited to visits to the house at weekends, most but not all weekends over the relevant time. Some of the matters complained of were clearly not caused by the breach of contract — for example the interference with the use of bath and WC caused by work to the plumbing which the plaintiffs chose to carry out at the same time as repair to the flooring.

Further, as explained in the judgment, the plaintiffs, finding that they had sufficient money to do so, decided to carry out work going far beyond the works the subject of the action. The judge held that the distress and inconvenience alleged by the plaintiffs was not to be discounted at all because he accepted, as sensible and well founded, the explanation by Mr Watts of his decision. For my part, while I have no doubt that it was a sensible and well founded decision for Mr Watts to do all the other work which he had decided to do at the same time as the repairs in respect of unreported defects, it does not seem to me thereby to be demonstrated that the physical discomfort and inconvenience throughout the period of work was caused by the failure to report those defects. It is clear that by 1987 the plaintiffs' earnings had risen and were rising. They decided that they would decorate and refurbish the house to a high standard. The need to do the repairs to unreported defects was not the reason why all the work was done when it was done. Indeed the need to carry out the unreported defects was seen by Mr Watts as delaying the process of refurbishment in the course of which the repairs of many other defects, of which there was no failure to give warning, were carried out. It is difficult, in my judgment, to be confident as a matter of probability that such physical discomfort as there was over the period of six months in 1988 was caused by the breach of contract of the defendant as contrasted with the decision of the plaintiffs to refurbish and redecorate the house. It is not clear to me that in any real sense the plaintiffs had to live in the house at weekends: their decision to do so appears to have resulted largely from their view that it was necessary for them to supervise personally all the work which they were having done.

The judge, however, accepted the plaintiffs' evidence and was not caused to doubt that all their complaints were caused by that breach of contract. It does not seem that the factual basis for the plaintiffs' claims to general damages was examined in any close detail at the trial. The right course, in my view, is for this court, accepting and applying the principle that damages for mental distress resulting from the physical consequence of such a breach of contract should be modest, to accept the judge's finding that, during the weekends over a period of eight months, there was discomfort from the physical circumstances of living in the house caused by the presence of the plaintiffs during the carrying out of repairs in respect of unreported defects. I reject the suggestion that, in comparing the proper awards in other cases of discomfort in a plaintiff's only home, there should be allowed, in respect of discomfort at weekends in an expensive second home, a comparatively larger sum. The proper approach is to fix a modest sum for the amount of physical discomfort endured having regard to the period of time over which it was endured. I would not take into account, as did the judge, in fixing the general damages, anything in respect of the plaintiffs' expenditure on a holiday in Scotland. There was no claim to loss of use. Any vexation in respect of taking a holiday away from the second home is not associated with physical discomfort in that home.

I would award to each plaintiff, since it has not been suggested that there is any basis for distinguishing between them, general damages in the sum of £750.

The award of interest.

In my judgment there is no ground for interfering with the judge's decision that interest at the rate of 15% should be awarded on the damages for financial loss. Mr Jackson's submission was that, the rate customarily awarded is the short-term investment account rate: reference was made to the *Supreme Court Practice,* volume 1, paragraph 6/2/16 at sub-paragraph (4); and that the judge erred in awarding a flat rate of 15% which was the same as the Judgment Act rate.

The award of interest at 15% was, in my judgment, within the judge's discretion and it is not shown that he misdirected himself or went wrong in principle in taking that rate. The facts that that rate was the same as the judgment rate, and was higher than the short term interest account rates over the relevant period, do not cause to be wrong the selection of that rate as the appropriate rate on the facts of this case: see the judgment of Nicholls LJ in *Pinnock* v *Wilkins:* unreported, 23 January 1990.

I would, accordingly, allow this appeal to the extent described above.

BINGHAM LJ: I am in complete agreement with the judgment of Ralph Gibson LJ which I have read in draft. I would allow the appeal to the extent he indicates for the reasons he gives. Since we are in part differing from the learned trial judge, who considered the matter with great care, I shall briefly give my own reasons.

(1) *Diminution in value or cost of repairs?*

The restitutory or compensatory principle which underlies the award of damages in contract is not open to question. Since it is ultimately a question of fact what sum of money is necessary to put a particular plaintiff in the position he would have been in if the particular defendant had properly performed the contract in question, I would accept Mr Naughton's contention that the measure of damages cannot be governed by an inflexible rule of law to be applied in all cases irrespective of the particular facts and regardless of whether or not such measure gives effect to the underlying principle. But this does not mean that there may not be sound *prima facie* rules to be applied in the ordinary run of cases. Examples may be found in sections 51(3) and 53(3) of the Sale of Goods Act 1979: these are only *prima facie* rules, but they reflect the same underlying principle and they govern cases to which they are not shown to be inapplicable. In the present field, by which I mean the purchase of houses by private buyers in reliance on a negligent survey of structure or condition, *Phillips* v *Ward* [1956] 1 WLR 471; 4 BLR 142 has been generally thought to lay down and in my view did lay down a prima facie rule for measuring damages. The crucial question is whether that *prima facie* rule was, as the judge held, inapplicable to the facts of the present case.

I do not think so. In *Phillips* v *Ward,* as in the present case, the cost of repairs exceeded the diminution in value. The Court of Appeal there pointed out that if the plaintiff received the house (for which he had paid £25,000) and £7,000 (the cost of repairs) he would in effect have obtained the house for £18,000. But the value of the house in the defective state in which it had actually been was £21,000, and had the defendant properly performed his contract the plaintiff could not have bought at any lower price. An award of £7,000 would not therefore have put him in the same position as if the defendant had properly performed his contract. It would have improved his position to the extent of £3,000 and thus put him in an advantageous position he could never have enjoyed had the defendant properly performed.

The same simple approach applies here. The plaintiffs paid £177,500, the value of the house as it was represented to be. The value of the house in its actual condition was £162,500, a difference of £15,000. The actual cost of repairs was (in rounded up figures) £34,000. If the plaintiff were to end up with the house and an award of £34,000 damages he would have obtained the house for £143,500. But even if the defendant had properly performed his contract this bargain was never on offer. The effect of the award is not to put the plaintiffs in the same position as if the defendant had properly performed but in a much better one.

I would be willing to accept, as Romer LJ did in *Phillips* v *Ward,* that if, on learning of the true state of the house, the plaintiffs had at once moved out and sold, they might well have been able to recover the costs thrown away in addition to the diminution in value. But these plaintiffs, no doubt for good reason, did not do that. They stayed and did the repairs. But the quantum of their claim would in theory be the same whether they had actually done and paid for the repairs or not, and if they had not the figures demonstate a clear windfall profit. If, on learning of the defects which should have been but were not reported, a purchaser decides (for whatever reason) to retain the house and not move out and sell, I would question whether any loss he thereafter suffers, at least in the ordinary case, can be laid at the door of the contract-breaker.

In the course of interesting and wide-ranging argument, a number of hypothetical situations were suggested in which the *prima facie* rule might be ousted or call for variation. I think it is wise to leave such cases for decision until they arise. I can see nothing in the present case to take it outside the *prima facie* rule in *Phillips* v *Ward*, and that is enough to resolve this issue in the defendant's favour.

(2) *Damages for distress and inconvenience.*
A contract-breaker is not in general liable for any distress, frustration, anxiety, displeasure, vexation, tension or aggravation which his breach of contract may cause to the innocent party. This rule is not, I think, founded on the assumption that such reactions are not foreseeable, which they surely are or may be, but on considerations of policy.

But the rule is not absolute. Where the very object of a contract is to provide pleasure, relaxation, peace of mind or freedom from molestation, damages will be awarded if the fruit of the contract is not provided or if the contrary result is procured instead. If the law did not cater for this exceptional category of case it would be defective. A contract to survey the condition of a house for a prospective purchaser does not, however, fall within this exceptional category.

In cases not falling within this exceptional category, damages are in my view recoverable for physical inconvenience and discomfort caused by the breach and mental suffering directly related to that inconvenience and discomfort. If those effects are foreseeably suffered during a period when defects are repaired I am prepared to accept that they sound in damages even though the cost of the repairs is not recoverable as such. But I also agree that awards should be restrained, and that the awards in this case far exceeded a reasonable award for the injury shown to have been suffered. I agree with the figures which Ralph Gibson LJ proposes to substitute.

(3) *Interest.*
Since the award of interest on damages is intended to compensate a plaintiff for being kept out of money lawfully due to him, there is much to be said for applying a rate of interest which reflects the cost or value of money over the relevant period rather than a flat rate fixed under the Judgment Act which has remained fixed over a number of years despite fluctuations in interest rates during that time. But the choice of an interest rate is discretionary and the judgment of Nicholls LJ in *Pinnock* v *Wilkins* (unreported, 23 January 1990) precludes the argument that choice of the Judgment Act rate of 15% is a challengeable exercise of discretion. On this point the judge's ruling cannot be disturbed.

THE PRESIDENT: I have had the advantage of reading in draft the judgments of Ralph Gibson LJ and Bingham LJ. I am in complete agreement with their conclusions.

The measure of damages in this case is governed by the principle clearly stated in *Phillips* v *Ward* [1956] 1 WLR 471; 4 BLR 142 and reaffirmed in *Perry* v *Sidney Phillips & Son* [1982] 1 WLR 1297; 22 BLR 120. I agree that the appeal should be allowed on this head as proposed by Ralph Gibson LJ and Bingham LJ.

I further agree that the quantum of damage awarded for "distress and inconvenience" was greatly excessive and that the sums proposed by Ralph Gibson LJ should be substituted. As to the appeal on the question of the rate of interest, I also agree that this was within the judge's discretion and should not be disturbed.

I therefore agree that the appeal should be allowed to the extent proposed by Ralph Gibson LJ and Bingham LJ.

NOTE

PAMELA SYRETT v CARR & NEAVE (a firm)

Queen's Bench Division
Official Referees' Business

31 July 1990 *His Honour Judge Bowsher QC*

JUDGE BOWSHER QC: The plaintiff claims damages for negligence against a surveyor arising out of a survey of a property known as Wootton Old Farm, Wootton, Hampshire. It is a very bad case of negligence, and indeed so bad that in the absence of any evidence from the surveyor who conducted the survey (Mr Carr), it is difficult to see how the errors were made. By the end of the trial there was no contest on liability except with regard to certain details.

The plaintiff works in the business of property management, based in London. Her husband is engaged in a number of businesses including a security company which among other things sells burglar alarms.

In 1986, the plaintiff and her husband were living with their seven year old son in a large five bed-roomed flat in London. They decided to change their life style by selling their large flat and in its place buying a large country house and a small London flat. They wanted spacious accommodation because they wanted to have schoolfriends of their son to stay (to compensate for his being an only child), they wanted to accommodate his nanny, and they wanted to entertain friends and business acquaintances. In addition, the plaintiff and her son both ride horses and her husband engages in other sports, and they wanted to extend these activities.

The plaintiff grew up in the country near Winchester, and so she looked at three or four properties in Hampshire. She then became attracted to Wootton Old Farm. Everyone is agreed that this is an exceptionally attractive building in an excellent position on the edge of the New Forest, with two acres of formal garden and another two acres of paddock. Parts of the house date from the seventeenth century. The plaintiff negotiated a price of £300,000 subject to contract and subject to survey. She had a budget of £100,000 to make improvements to the property.

The plaintiff accepted that in a house of this age there would be matters which required attention, but before she entered into a contract she wanted to be assured that there were no items of major expenditure which would affect her decision to purchase. Accordingly, she instructed the defendants, as a firm recommended as having local expertise, to make a limited survey.

By a letter dated 4 September 1986, the defendants agreed to "make a survey of the main walls and roof only of the property". An attendance note of Mr Carr confirms that he agreed to consider main walls, roof, and damp. I am in no doubt that damp was to be included in his survey.

Mr Carr reported on 12 September 1986. His report contained the statement, which I find reflects the agreement between the parties, that "my survey is restricted to items of major expenditure which would affect your intention to purchase or the price offered". There were in fact major defects in the property including a very bad infestation with death watch beetle, movement in some of the walls, and severe damp in some places. The favourite food of the death watch beetle is damp oak, and dampness goes hand in hand with deathwatch beetle in houses where there are oak beams. The defendants reported some minor problems with damp, but not the main problems, and otherwise failed to report on the major problems. One of the plaintiff's complaints relates to some outbuildings which were also infested with death watch beetle. Liability for those outbuildings was contested on the basis that, as was the fact, they were outside the defendants' brief. Late in the trial it was conceded by an expert witness called for the defendants that once a prudent surveyor had seen the death watch beetle infestation in the house (as he should have done), he should have warned his client to investigate the outbuildings.

The plaintiff was very unfortunate that she was not recommended to consult a different local surveyor, Mr Richard McNeil, who gave evidence for the defendants. He verified two witness statements, one dated 2 April 1990, and the other dated 24 July 1990, the day before he gave oral evidence. In neither of those statements did he disclose the information put forward in oral examination in chief that he himself had inspected this property in October 1976 and again in September 1980, on instructions from a building society which was considering on the first occasion a re-mortgage and on the second occasion a further advance against the property. In his examination in chief he did not disclose the facts (no doubt because he was not asked) elicited by me during re-examination that on each occasion he saw death watch beetle and recommended to the building society that treatment to the timbers and damproofing should be carried out. Mr McNeil did say in his first witness statement that, "I have never inspected a property of this age which has not suffered from an infestation of woodworm and/or death watch beetle". In the light of information either known or available to them, it is surprising that the defendants contested liability for so long. That is a matter which has no relevance to the issue of damages, but it might be relevant on costs. The defendants did make admissions on the first day of the trial in the following terms:

> "The defendants failed adequately to inspect the property and to see the evidence of death watch beetle and its effects on the timber in various parts thereof, in particular in the roof void, the attic bedrooms and the first floor bedrooms.
>
> The defendants failed in their written report of 12 September 1986 to report to the plaintiff the evidence of deathwatch beetle in the premises and to warn her that the full extent thereof could not be determined by a survey such as this, that it might be extensive, and that remedial work might be required, and to advise her that a specialist inspection would be prudent.
>
> In reliance upon the defendants' written report of 12 September 1986, the plaintiff contracted to and did purchase the property for the sum of £300,000."

Later, at 2 pm on the second day of the hearing, the defendants by their counsel admitted that they no longer resisted liability in respect of the damp-proof course with the exception of the damp proof course in the kitchen. Consultants had recommended that a special damp proof course be inserted in all the walls of the old part of the house. Part of those old walls were in the kitchen. On behalf of the defendants it was said that there was no evidence of damp in that particular room. However, the kitchen fitments impeded the fullest damp tests, and in any event, when damp is found in all the other old walls of the house it seems only prudent to extend damp-proofing to the one room in which damp has not been positively found.

The plaintiff stated in evidence, "Had I known of the death watch beetle infestation, I would not have purchased the property but would have purchased another suitable property in the area". I accept that evidence. The whole purpose of the survey was to discover whether there were any major defects which would affect the decision to buy.

Relying on the survey, the plaintiff exchanged contracts on 1 October 1986. The price was £300,000 which all concerned are agreed was a fair market price for the house if it has been as described in the defendants' report. The conveyance was completed on 6 February 1987, and the plaintiff and her family moved in during that month. After exchange of contracts, she put her large London flat on the market, but did not manage to sell it until June 1989. After selling the flat, the plaintiff rented a small one and a half bedroomed house in London. Meanwhile, the plaintiff had discovered the death watch beetle infestation in her house in the country.

Quite reasonably, she decided that they would live in the house for a while to get the feel of the house before spending the budgeted sum on improvements. During the period after moving in and before alterations were planned in detail, there was one disturbing incident. In the autumn of 1987, Mr Syrett lit an oil fired Aga and then oil fumes were smelt in the bedroom above. The plaintiff had the chimneys investigated and was advised that the linings of the flues had perished and needed replacing and they were replaced at a cost of £3,569.00.

In October 1988, the plaintiff engaged Mr Peter Young, an architect, to advise on alterations to the house. When he visited in October 1988, the plaintiff mentioned to him her concern about some orange dust which fell on the covers of the beds in the attic bedrooms. Mr Young advised a survey which he was instructed to conduct. That survey revealed a long standing and severe attack of death watch beetle, extensive damp, and distortion of the walls, in particular of the west gable wall and of the chimney built up against it.

Mr Young advised that work should be done at a cost, including VAT and fees, of about £150,000. At the trial he accepted that those works were not necessarily related to the defendants' negligent report. After discussions with the quantity surveyor instructed by the defendants, Mr Rennie, he accepted a cheaper way of doing some of the work, deleted some items, reduced others and reached some compromises. His final figure was £77,997.44. Mr Rennie put forward a total of £41,467.39.

The work has not been put in hand. The plaintiff said that she would like the work to be done as soon as possible. She did not discover the problem until October 1988, so she could not have had the work done before then. Until the sale of the London flat in June 1989 she was short of funds because she had borrowed a substantial amount of money to make the purchase on the basis that she could let the house if there was any delay in selling the flat, and once the problem had come to light, letting the house became impossible because the falling dust left only two bedrooms habitable. She also has the problem that until she knows the outcome of the litigation, she does not know how much she can spend on the house. I find that she has acted entirely reasonably. I am sure that if she could have done the work she would have done so because the state of the house has been and is totally disruptive of her family life and causes her great stress and worry. She and her husband cannot entertain their friends and business clients, and she cannot, as she would wish, have her son's friends to stay. Since the sale of the London flat the bulk of their furniture went first into storage and then in packing cases into the house making many more rooms unusable. When instructions are given for the work to begin, a month's notice will have to be given (this being a listed property) and the work will take eighteen weeks. (There is a dispute about the length of time that will be taken, but that is my finding.) It is agreed that when the work begins, the plaintiff and her family will have to move out of the house, causing more inconvenience and more expense in the form of removal and storage costs and rental of alternative accommodation. All of this damage is a natural and probable consequence of the defendants' negligence.

By whatever principle damages are calculated, the cost of repair is relevant in this case. I therefore turn to consider the costs of repair. This case has given rise to more detailed consideration of costings than any other I have heard. In a schedule of 166 items, many were agreed, under some pressure from me, but many other items remained in dispute. Mr Young's original figures were on the generous side and Mr Rennie's original figures were on the mean side. But whereas Mr Young moved very substantially from his original position, Mr Rennie was unwilling to budge from certain contentions of substance even though his position seems to me to be plainly unsustainable. I will give some examples.

Example 1: Mr Young's figures contain a contingency allowance of 5%, which is fairly modest in the circumstances. Mr Rennie contended that as the property had been opened up no allowance should be made for contingencies, and stuck to that position even after he had admitted that 66% of the timbers in the roof had not been examined because of the limits on the opening up.

Example 2: There was a difference between Mr Young and Mr Rennie as to the cost of replacement timber. This came down to a difference over some floor boards. Mr Young said that some temporary floor boards had been put in and they should be replaced by boards which matched the original boards. Mr Rennie admitted that the boards in question were white in appearance and were 6″ wide while the original boards were 10″ wide and were of a pleasing reddish colour which would polish up pleasantly if anyone wished to treat them in that way. I find it surprising that it should be suggested that a period listed house should be repaired in the way proposed by Mr Rennie.

Example 3: Specialists advised that a new damp-proof course should be inserted in all the oldest walls of the house, including the kitchen and further advised that to have the advantage of their guarantee the plaster on the inside walls should be hacked off and replaced. Mr Rennie contended that as no damp had actually been measured in the kitchen the damp-proofing treatment should not be taken into the kitchen and there should be no charge for removing kitchen units from that room and there should be a reduction in the specialists' charges. I have already given my reasons for rejecting Mr Rennie's contentions in that regard.

Example 4: Mr Rennie gave evidence from personal experience that oil fumes were commonly given off by an Aga until it reached its maximum efficiency on heating up. But for the plaintiff it is contended that for the smell to get into the bedroom there must have been a crack in the chimney and in the wall between the chimney and the bedroom. No one has ever seen such a crack, either internally or externally in any chimney. There may be such a crack between floor and ceiling and that seems the most likely route for the fumes to have got into the bedroom. The chimneys are parts of the main walls and the chimney in question is attached to the west gable which has undoubtedly moved as has also the chimney with it. Had Mr Carr noted the movement in the gable wall and this chimney he should have suspected cracking and should have conducted a smoke test on the chimney. He would then have seen smoke going into the bedroom and would have realised by further inspection that the lining had crumbled away. That would have led him to an inspection of the interior of the other chimneys and he would have discovered that their linings also had crumbled.

Example 5: There are some outbuildings which contain a quantity of oak which needs repair and treatment. Mr Rennie maintained that the estimated cost of the work to the outbuildings should be deleted from the plaintiffs' claim because the outbuildings were not included in the defendants' brief. He took up this stance even though he readily admitted in cross-examination that if a prudent surveyor found a severe attack of death watch beetle in the main house (as he should have done) he ought to have advised his client that the outbuildings should be investigated. I find that the costs of work to the outbuildings should be included in the costs of repair for the purpose of this action.

Having regard to my findings as between Mr Young and Mr Rennie on the differences between them which could be and were adequately tested at the trial, I have no hesitation in finding that Mr Young's evidence was more persuasive than Mr Rennie's and should be preferred also on those points where the differences could not be adequately tested.

There was an issue between Mr Young and Mr Rennie as to the length of time that would be taken for the work. The time taken to do the work is relevant to consequential losses such as rental of alternative accommodation. Mr Young invited tenders from ten builders. In the event, after four had tendered, only one was willing to do the work. That builder estimated that the time to be taken would be twenty-five weeks. Mr Young beat him down to twenty weeks. Mr Young says that allowing for the fact that he has agreed certain omissions in the work, the time taken should be reduced to eighteen weeks. Mr Rennie says that because of the omissions the length of the work should be reduced to ten weeks. Mr Young justifies his estimate by saying that it is not right to look at the difference between his original estimate in terms of money and compare that with his present estimate. The major item of reduction is due to a concession made by him that it would not be necessary to take off the roof. While the roof was being taken off, other work could have been in progress, certainly on the ground floor and probably also on upper floors of the house in rooms not directly under the working position of the roofers at any one time. On this point also I prefer Mr Young's evidence to that of Mr Rennie and find that the best estimate of the time to be taken on the work would be eighteen weeks.

I therefore find that the costs of repair in July 1990 would be in the sum now assessed by Mr Young, £77,997.44, and that the time to be taken to do the work is likely to be eighteen weeks. The precise make-up of Mr Young's figure is set out in exhibit P1 and I need not refer to it in this judgment.

Other costs ancillary to the repairs are as follows:

1 Removal, storage, and insurance of furniture for eighteen weeks. The plaintiffs claim £6,400 which seems to me to be reasonable.

2 Rental of alternative premises at an agreed price of £277 per week which for eighteen weeks would be £4,986.

3 Removal, storage, and reinstallation of a burglar alarm system. This system is very sophisticated and delicate and would suffer badly from dust and from the vibration caused during works on the premises. Having heard the evidence of Mr Syrett, whose company installed the system, it seems to me to be reasonable that the system should be removed before work is started. This is an expense which the plaintiff incurs as a result of going into the property before the defects were discovered. Mr Syrett very fairly accepts that the number of hours charged in his company's estimate appears inflated.

I accept the number of hours put forward by the plaintiffs' counsel as reasonable and I assess the cost of this item at £750.

4 There is a claim for recovery of the fee paid for the report on the basis that it was useless. The plaintiff is entitled to £253 under this head.

5 Damages are also claimed for inconvenience and distress.

6 The plaintiff also claims interest.

I turn to consider the basis on which damages should be assessed.

The costs of repair formed part of the considerations of both experts who gave evidence of value. In addition to being Professor of Building Surveying at the Department of Construction Management in the University of Reading, Professor Hollis is also a director of the very old established firm of Baxter Payne and Leppard. He has considerable experience dealing in London with clients who are looking for what he calls "more interesting houses" outside London but as far afield as Wiltshire, Gloucestershire, Hampshire and Sussex. He sees that market as a whole and to that extent has the advantage of the surveyor called for the defendants, Mr Richard McNeil, to whom I have already referred. Mr McNeil, a director of Cornerstone Professional, practising from Lymington, has the advantage of detailed local knowledge. Mr McNeil tends to go no further than ten miles from his office for valuation. Wootton Old Farm is about six miles from his office.

Both surveyors took the purchase price of £300,000 as the starting point, it being agreed that was a fair valuation for the house as described by the defendants. Professor Hollis then took the costs of repair given by Mr Young, £70,000, and using a method accepted by the defendants, projected that figure back to give an equivalent cost for the same work being done in

September 1986. That figure he calculated as £52,000. Considering the general hypothetical purchaser who had knowledge of the defects, the costs of repair would be directly relevant. If works can be delayed they are not a direct deduction, but here they could not be delayed, and the purchaser would know that entry into occupation would be delayed. Professor Hollis took that delay as sixteen weeks. As a result of the delay the purchaser would be faced with the additional costs of holding two homes (either financing costs through delayed sale of his existing home or rental of alternative accommodation). In addition, Professor Hollis said that one should take into consideration the risk that the repairs "may damage the wisteria that is so much a part of the character of the south elevation of this property". That wisteria is well established and obviously old and could not be replaced in its present glory for many years. It is notable that Mr McNeil also said, "Works on this scale could destroy much of the essential character of a property of this age and type". On the basis of no evidence, it was suggested by counsel for the defendants in his closing speech that there might be an element of "betterment" arising out of the repairs: but even disregarding the legal objections to that submission, it seems more likely that the repairs will damage the overall value of the house rather than the contrary. Professor Hollis described the cost of repairs as the "core" of the deductions, which in this case would be deducted in totality, but there would not be a 100% deduction for what he called the peripherals.

Taking these matters into account, Professor Hollis gave his opinion that £55,000 would be deducted from the £300,000 market value, giving a value for the house in its actual state in September, 1986 of £245,000.

Mr McNeil on the other hand took Mr Rennie's repair figure of £41,000 and adjusted that to a repair cost of £29,000 in September 1986. On the basis of the property not being opened up, and there being a measure of uncertainty about the figure, he estimated a market price of £275,000, allowing for a contingency of about 15%. Taking the same figure, which Mr Rennie adhered to after opening up, he eliminated the 15% contingency and estimated a market price of £285,000, which he later revised to £283,000. He said that a minimum "bedrock" price would be £265,000, and that would be the value if Mr Young's figure of £78,000 for repairs were to be accepted. Mr McNeil based that opinion on the rarity of properties of this type in the New Forest and on the state of the market at the time. He described market conditions in the New Forest in the last quarter of 1986 as "good". Professor Hollis said that the market generally was "reasonably firm", "steady", "not buoyant".

I prefer the evidence of Professor Hollis. The art of valuation is well supported by local knowledge. But the market for this type of house is very much larger than the ten mile radius around Mr McNeil's office. Since Mr McNeil regards this type of property as being so rare in his area, he must have comparatively little experience of dealings in such property compared with Professor Hollis who has as his clients many potential purchasers for this type of property. The vendor must have known that potential purchasers for his property would not necessarily limit their search for a house to his area. Moreover, it is difficult to believe that Mr McNeil's two reports to the building society had not been drawn to his attention and in September he had men working on the roof from scaffolding. Only a sentimental fool with money to burn would buy a house for £265,000 knowing that he would have to spend £78,000 on it to make it worth at most £300,000, and probably less due to possible damage to the character of the house by the works. The hypothetical buyer should not be taken to be a sentimental fool, because there are not many sentimental fools able to retain their money for long enough to buy houses for £300,000 at 1986 prices. Certainly the plaintiff is a hard headed businesswoman who would not go in for that sort of deal. Although she was attracted to the Winchester area and to this house in particular, she would not have bought this house at all had she known about the death watch beetle, and that would have been the view of the ordinary hypothetical purchaser who was looking for a home rather than a property developer looking for a house to do up for resale. The property developer would certainly not buy at a price which could not show a profit.

The major item of the plaintiffs' costs is the cost of repairs. I have to decide whether those costs should be recoverable as a simple head of damages or whether I should award damages on the basis of diminution in value, which in this case is heavily influenced by the cost of repairs.

In a solicitor's negligence action, *County Personnel Ltd* v *Alan R Pulver & Co* [1987] 1 WLR 916 at page 925, Bingham LJ stated eight principles to be applied in assessing damages. The first four of those are of particular relevance in this case and are as follows:

> "(1) The overriding rule was stated by Lord Blackburn in *Livingstone* v *Rawyards Coal Co* (1880) 5 App Cas 25, 39, and has been repeated on countless occasions since: the measure of damages is
>
> > 'that sum of money which will put the party who has been injured, or who has suffered, in the same position as he would have been if he had not sustained the wrong for which he is now getting his compensation or reparation.'
>
> As Megaw LJ added in *Dodd Properties (Kent) Ltd* v *Canterbury City Council* [1980] 1 WLR 433, 451:
>
> > 'In any case of doubt, it is desirable that the judge, having decided provisionally as to the amount of damages, should, before finally deciding, consider whether the amount conforms with the requirement of Lord Blackburn's fundamental principle. If it appears not to conform, the judge should examine the question again to see whether the particular case falls within one of the exceptions of which Lord Blackburn gave examples, or whether he is obliged by some binding authority to arrive at a result which is inconsistent with fundamental principle.'
>
> (2) On the authorities as they stand the diminution in value rule appears almost always, if not always, to be appropriate where property is acquired following negligent advice by surveyors. Such cases as *Philips* v *Ward* [1956] 1 WLR 471; *Pilkington* v *Wood* [1953] Ch 770; *Ford* v *White & Co* [1964] 1 WLR 885 and *Perry* v *Sidney Philips & Son* [1982] 1 WLR 1297, lay down that rule and illustrate its application in cases involving both surveyors and solicitors.

(3) That is not, however, an invariable approach, at least in claims against solicitors, and should not be mechanistically applied in cases where it may appear inappropriate. In *Simple Simon Catering Ltd* v *Binstock Miller & Co* (1973) 228 EG 527 the Court of Appeal favoured a more general assessment taking account of the 'general expectation of loss'. In other cases the cost of repair or reinstatement may provide the appropriate measure: the *Dodd Properties* case [1980] 1 WLR 433, 456, *per* Donaldson LJ. In other cases the measure of damage may properly include the cost of making good the error of a negligent adviser: examples are found in *Braid* v *W L Highway & Sons* (1964) 191 EG 433, and *G + K Ladenbau (UK) Ltd* v *Crawley de Reya* [1978] 1 WLR 266.

(4) While the general rule undoubtedly is that damages for tort or breach of contract are assessed as at the date of breach (see for example, *Miliangos* v *George Frank (Textiles) Ltd* [1976] AC 433, 468, *per* Lord Wilberforce), this rule should not be mechanistically applied in circumstances where assessment at another date may more accurately reflect the overriding compensatory rule. The *Dodd Properties* case both affirms this principle and illustrates its application ..."

Following the guideline set out by Megaw LJ in the *Dodd Properties* case, it seems to me that the appropriate measure of damages to put the plaintiff in the same position as she would have been if she had not sustained the wrong is the cost of repairs plus the costs ancillary to those repairs plus compensation for the blight on her happiness since October 1988. If she had received a careful rather than a negligent report, she would not have bought this property and she would have bought a property which would have been worth what she paid for it and would not have required large expenditure in repairs and would have given her much enjoyment already. It does not seem to me that this approach falls within one of the exceptions mentioned by Lord Blackburn and I therefore turn to consider whether there is some binding authority which obliges me to arrive at some different result.

The two principal binding authorities which I have to consider are *Philips* v *Ward* [1956] 1 WLR 471 and *Perry* v *Sidney Phillips & Son* [1982] 1 WLR 1297. In *Philips* v *Ward*, the Court of Appeal held that *on the facts of that case* (see Morris LJ at page 476 line 5) the appropriate measure of damages was the difference in value between the value of the property as it was described in the defendants' report and the value as it should have been described. In that case, the difference in value was £4,000 and the cost of repairs at the time of purchase was £7,000. The work of repair had not been done by the date of the trial, and the Court of Appeal held on the facts of that case that it was not reasonable to have delayed doing the repair (*per* Morris LJ page 475). Both of those facts differ from the facts of the present case. The date when the infestation by death watch beetle was discovered in *Philips* v *Ward* is not clear from the report. In the statement of facts on page 471 it is stated that the plaintiff bought in June 1952 and moved in and "it was then found that the timbers of the house were badly affected by death watch beetle". The only reason for postponing the doing of the works put forward by the plaintiff appears to have been that the plaintiff wanted the property to be available for inspection at the date of the hearing. That reason was not surprisingly rejected by Morris LJ (page 475 first paragraph). I infer that the purchaser in *Philips* v *Ward* discovered the death watch beetle soon after moving into the property and he had a choice between selling the property again at its true value, making a loss which was less than the then cost of repairs, or doing the repairs. In those circumstances, to award as damages the cost of doing the repairs would have given him a benefit to which he was not entitled in the absence of a warranty from the surveyor as to the state of the property. That is not the case here where instant resale of the property would not have left the purchaser with a loss less than the cost of repairs and more importantly, the purchaser had no reason to make an instant sale of the property because she did not know of the defect until two years after moving in and by then she was so heavily involved with the proprty that it was reasonable for her to keep it and repair it. It seems to me to be wholly artificial to tell a plaintiff that her damage is to be measured in relation to a loss which she could have taken by making a sale two years before she learned that there was a loss to be realised. That does not seem to me to be what the Court of Appeal was saying in *Phillips* v *Ward* on the facts of that case.

In *Perry* v *Sidney Phillips* also, the defects unreported in the negligent report seem likely to have been discovered very soon after the plaintiff moved into the property. The defects were a leaking roof and a septic tank giving off an offensive smell (see page 1300 H). Again, the plaintiff had a choice of either cutting his loss by reselling or undertaking the necessary repairs. He chose not to resell until after the trial, and he did not have the means to undertake repairs. Oliver LJ in that case (at page 1304G) rejected a submission based on *Dodd Properties* [1980] 1 WLR 433 that the loss should "be assessed on the basis of some hypothetical value at the date of trial because the plaintiff has chosen — as he did in this case — to retain the property and not to cut his loss by reselling it". In the same case, at page 1302, Lord Denning MR said:

> "The general rule of law is that you assess the damages at the date of the breach so as to put the plaintiff in the same position as he would have been in if the contract had been properly performed. Even if the claim be laid in tort against the surveyor, the damages should be on the same basis."

If the plaintiff is unaware of the breach until two years after the breach took place there may be many reasons for not applying that general rule and in my judgment there are cogent reasons for not applying that general rule in this case. Those cogent reasons are that the plaintiff did not have an opportunity of cutting her losses at or about the date of purchase and that she has acted reasonably throughout and that all the expenses which I find she has suffered or is likely to suffer are natural and probable results of the negligent survey. The plaintiff did have an opportunity of cutting her losses two years after purchase of the property in October 1988, but in her circumstances at the time it seems to me to have been reasonable for her to decide not to do so, and in any event there is no evidence before me as to what would have been the financial results of her selling at that time.

Accordingly, to return to the words of Megaw LJ in *Dodd Properties*, I do not feel that I am "obliged by some binding authority to arrive at a result which is inconsistent with the fundamental principle".

I therefore hold that the plaintiff is entitled to damages comprising the cost of repairs together with the ancillary costs associated with those repairs and damages for distress and inconvenience together with return of the fee paid for the report.

The cost of repairs should be assessed as at the date when they are likely to be done, the plaintif having acted reasonably in delaying the repairs. That much is not in issue between the parties. But for the plaintiff it is submitted that the costs should be increased from the date they were estimated earlier in 1990 up to the date when the work is likely to be done to take account of the effects of inflation. For the defendants it is contended that builders, in particular builders in the Lymington area, are so short of work that it should be possible to negotiate with them to stick with the prices already agreed and given in evidence. I accept the defendants' evidence in that regard. The price of repairs should be the price given in evidence by Mr Young without adjustment.

The plaintiff claims damages for inconvenience and distress. She plainly is entitled to such damages on a scale which is not excessive but modest: see *per* Lord Denning MR in *Perry* v *Sidney Phillips* [1982] 1 WLR at 1302, 1303. A most helpful article by Miss Kim Franklin in (1988) *Construction Law Journal* at page 264 makes interesting comparisons between the misery caused by people being in an unsatisfactory home with the distress caused by ruined holidays and minor personal injuries. The plaintiff has been restrained in describing her distress and inconvenience, but it has been real, substantial, and prolonged, lasting from about October 1988 until early next year. It has been much more serious than a spoilt fortnight in Mallorca though not as bad as the experiences of some householders. I assess those damages on a moderate scale in the sum of £8,000.

The damages therefore are as follows:

1 Cost of repair	77,997.44
2 Removal, storage and insurance of furniture	6,349.70
3 Rental of alternative premises	4,986.00
4 Removal and reinstallation of burglar alarm	750.00
5 Fee paid for report	253.00
6 Damages for inconvenience and distress	8,000.00
	98,336.14

As none of those costs have yet been incurred, apart from items 5 and 6, I do not think it appropriate to award interest.

If, however, it should be held that I am wrong and that I should have awarded damages on the diminution in value approach, I would award damages and interest on that basis as follows:

1 Diminution in value	55,000.00
2 Interest from the date of contract 6 October 1986 to today at 15%	31,679.03
3 Removal storage and insurance of furniture 4 Rental of alternative premises	1,000.00
5 Rental and reinstallation of burglar alarm	750.00
6 Fee paid for report	253.00
7 Damages for inconvenience and distress	4,000.00
	92,682.03

The figures assessed for items 3. and 4. on this method of calculation are lower than on the first method of calculation because Professor Hollis took sixteen of the eighteen weeks of rental and storage into account in reaching his valuation figure, and one should not indulge in double counting. For the same reason, the damages for inconvenience and distress are lower.

Where damages are calculated on the basis of diminution in value they are calculated as at the date when the purchaser relies on the negligent advice by entering into a contract to purchase, and interest therefore runs from the same date: *Perry* v *Sidney Phillips* [1982] 1 WLR 1297 at 1301-1302.

Subject to corrections of my arithmetic, I therefore award to the plaintiff damages in the sum of £98,336.14 and no interest.

Index of Cases Reported in Volumes 1-54

Cases with company names are indexed under the first name, even where this is the forename of an individual – eg John Thompson Horseley Bridge Ltd under "J". Where, however, the company name includes initials the case is indexed under the surname – eg F G Minter under "M".

Index of Cases Referred to in Volume 54